MW00904700

# Alphabet Trace The Letters

## For Preschoolers

Ages
**3-5**+

## Little Monster

This Book Belongs To:

_____

_____

ALPHABET

# The Latter A

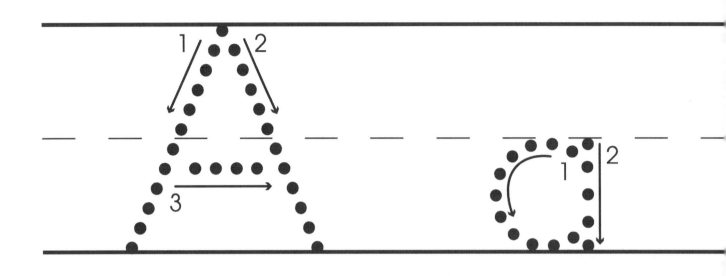

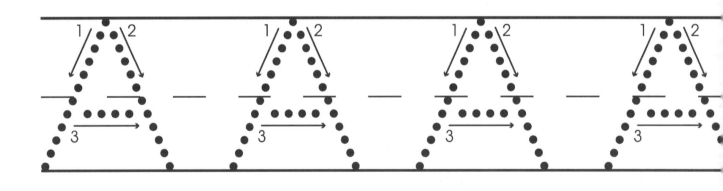

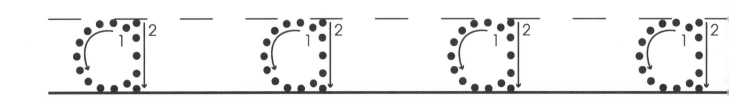

# A is for

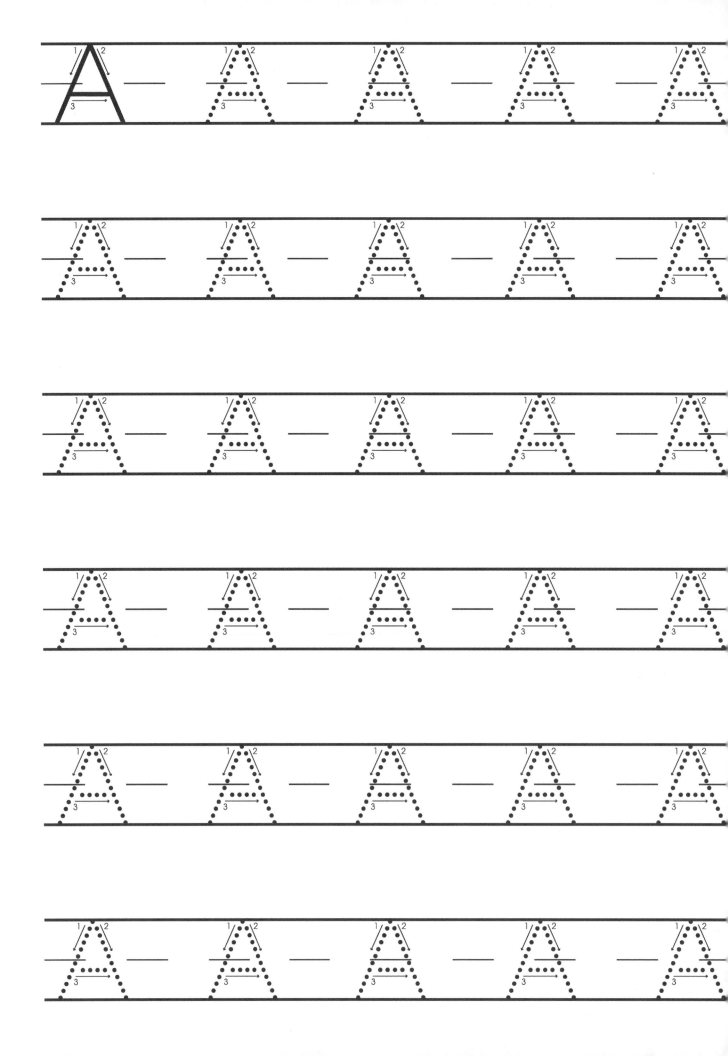

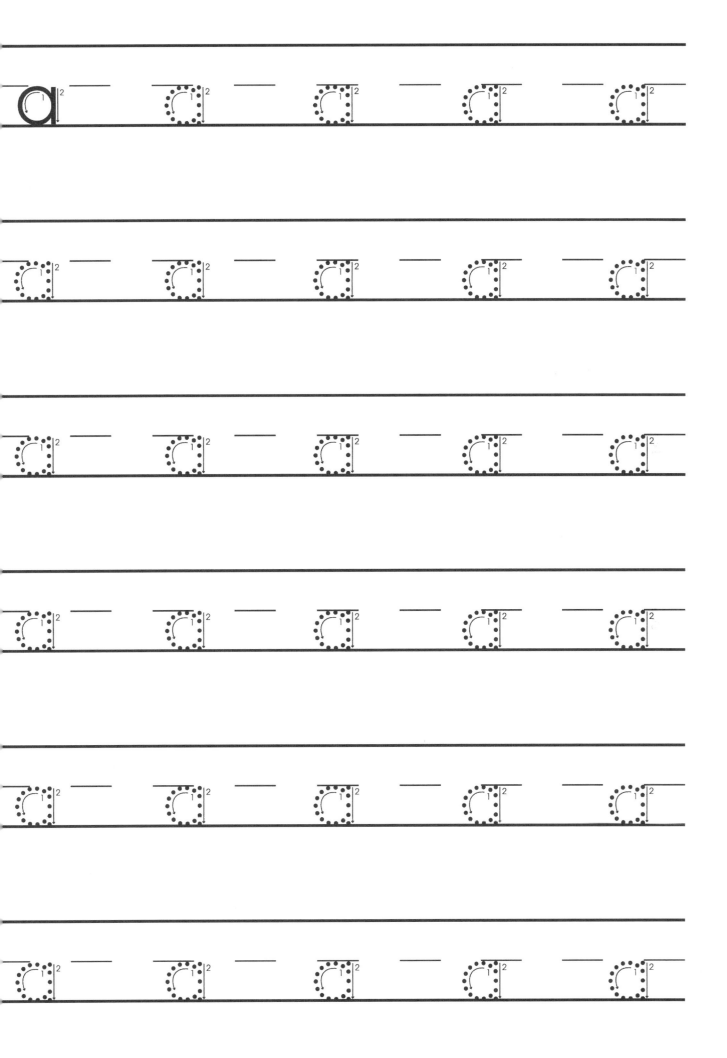

# The Latter B

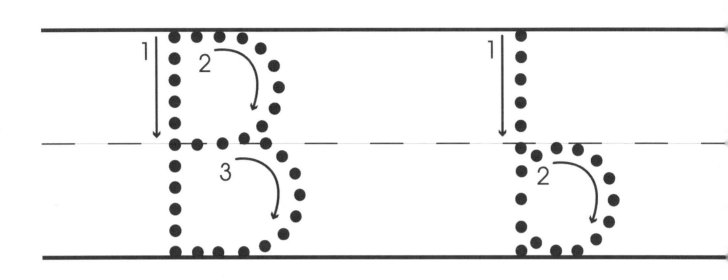

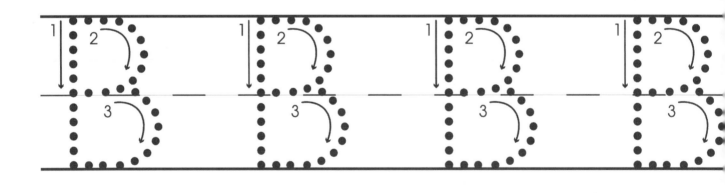

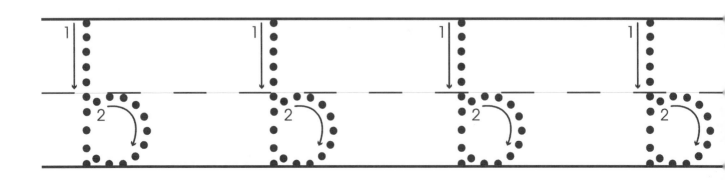

# B is for

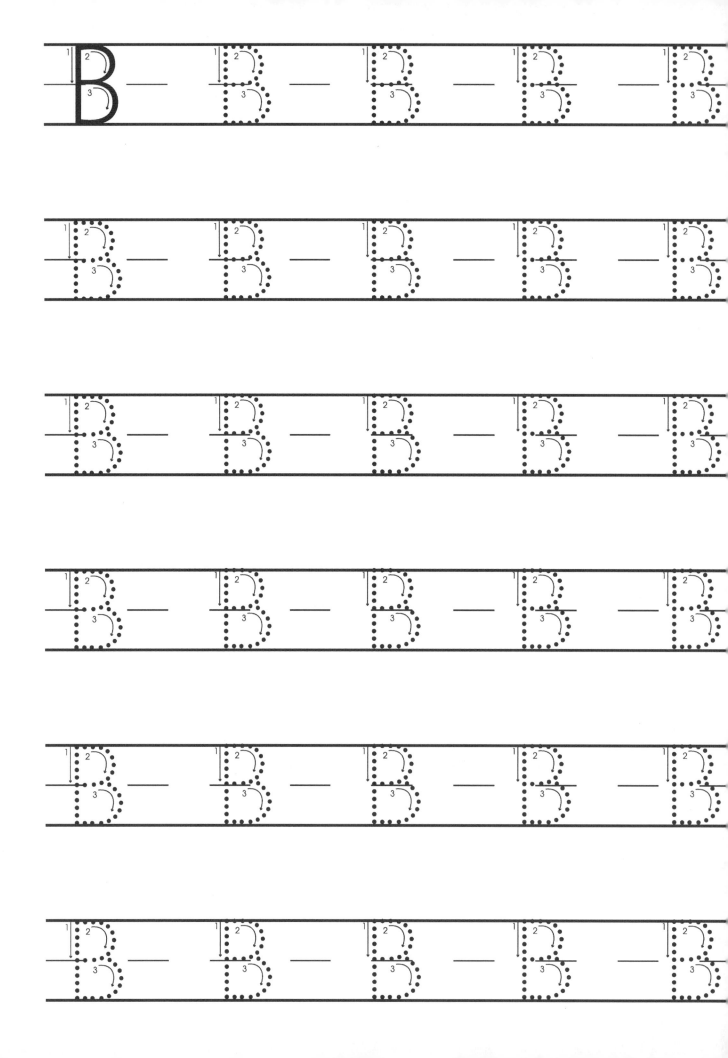

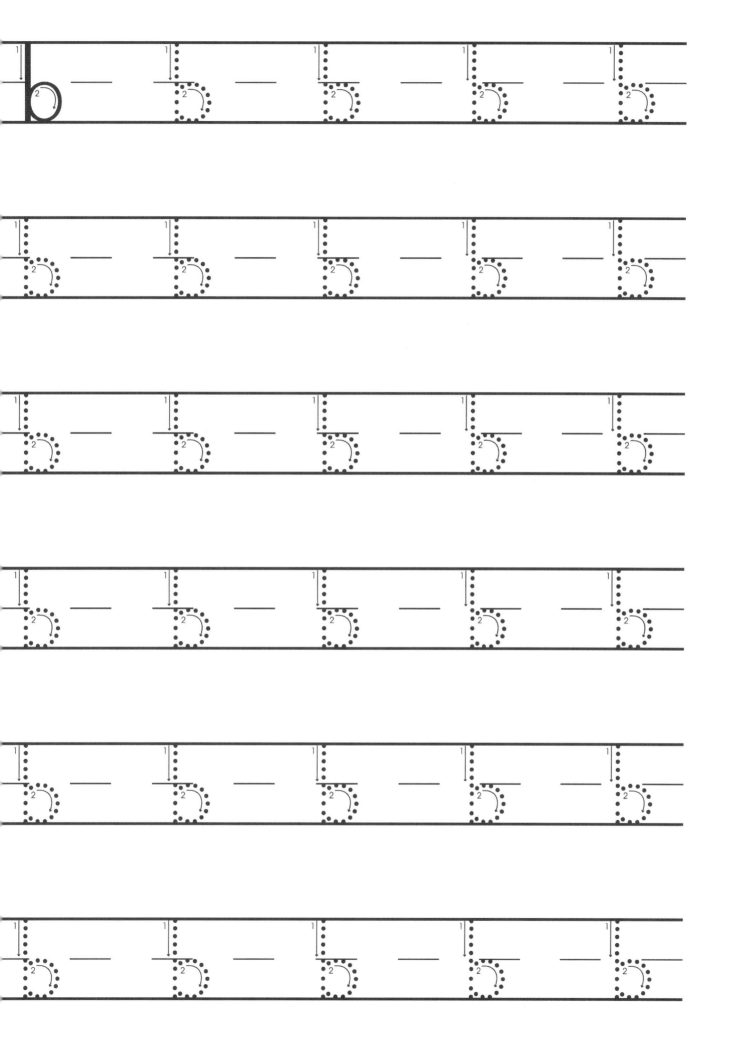

# The Latter C

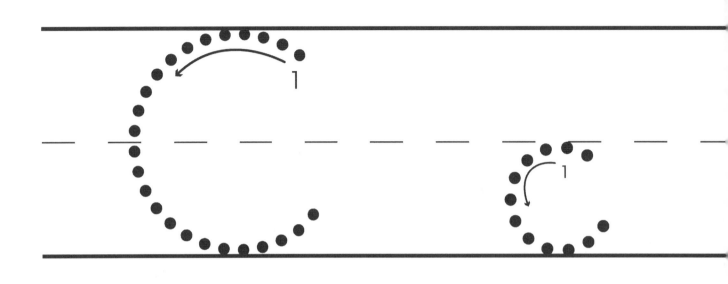

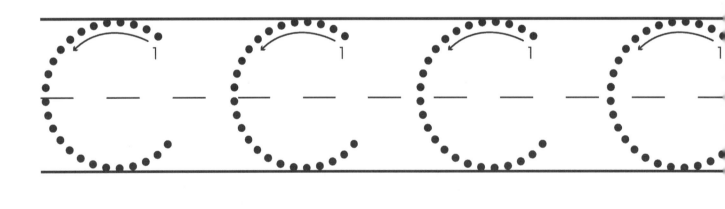

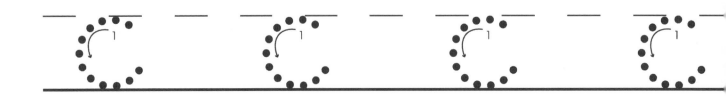

# C is for

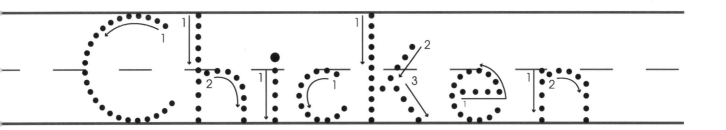

C C C C C

C C C C C

C C C C C

C C C C C

C C C C C

C C C C C

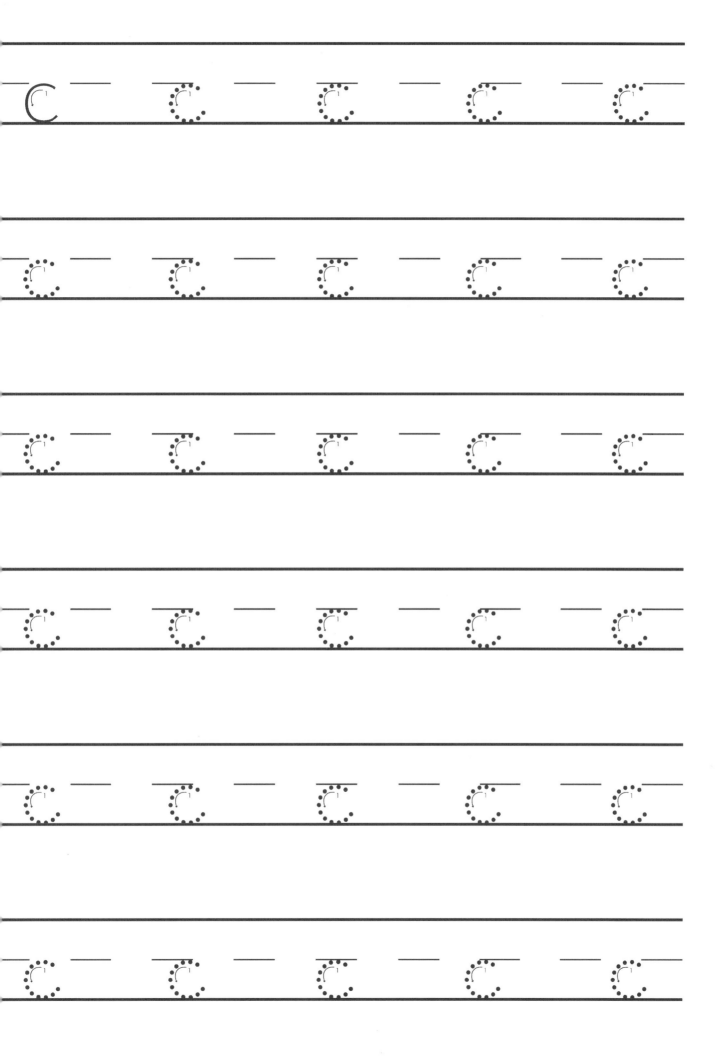

# The Latter D

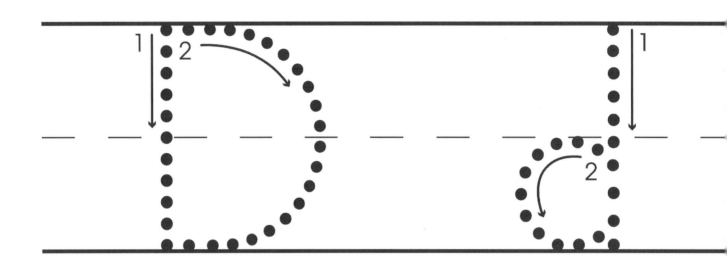

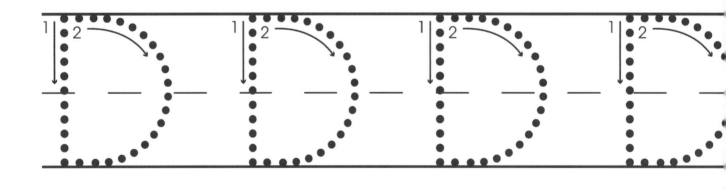

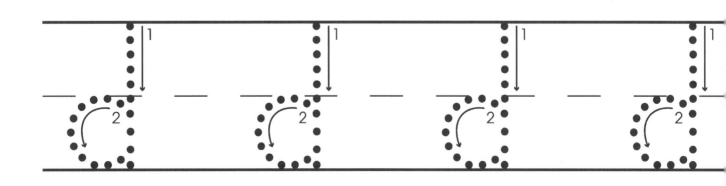

# D is for

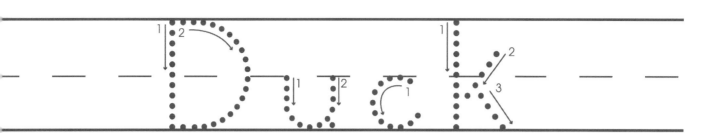

D

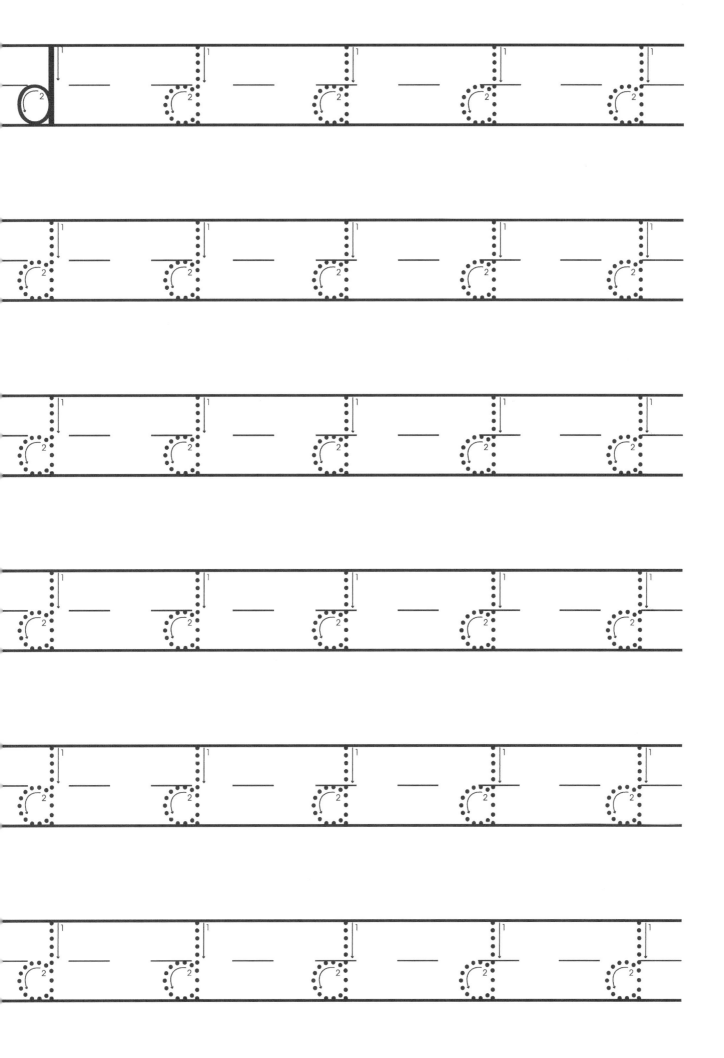

# The Latter E

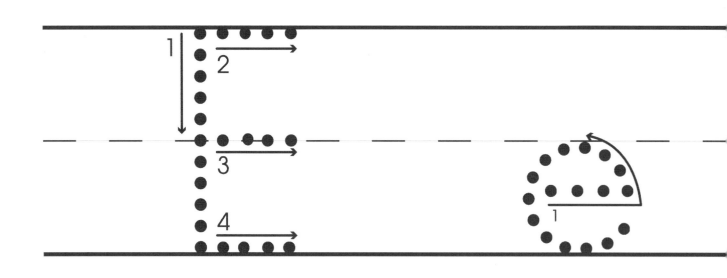

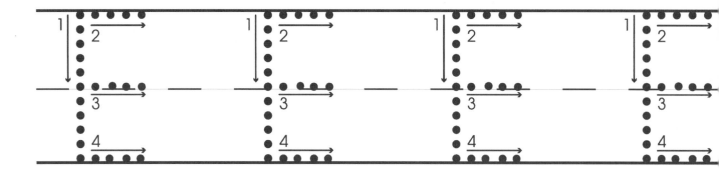

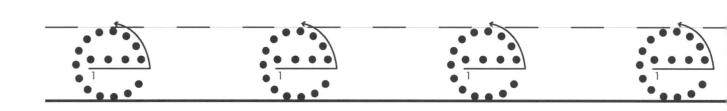

# E is for

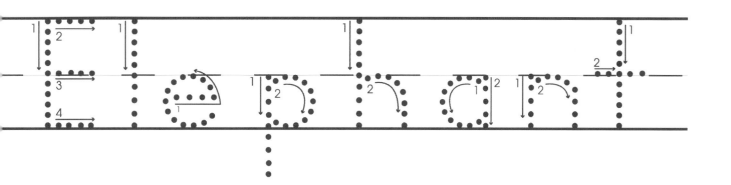

E

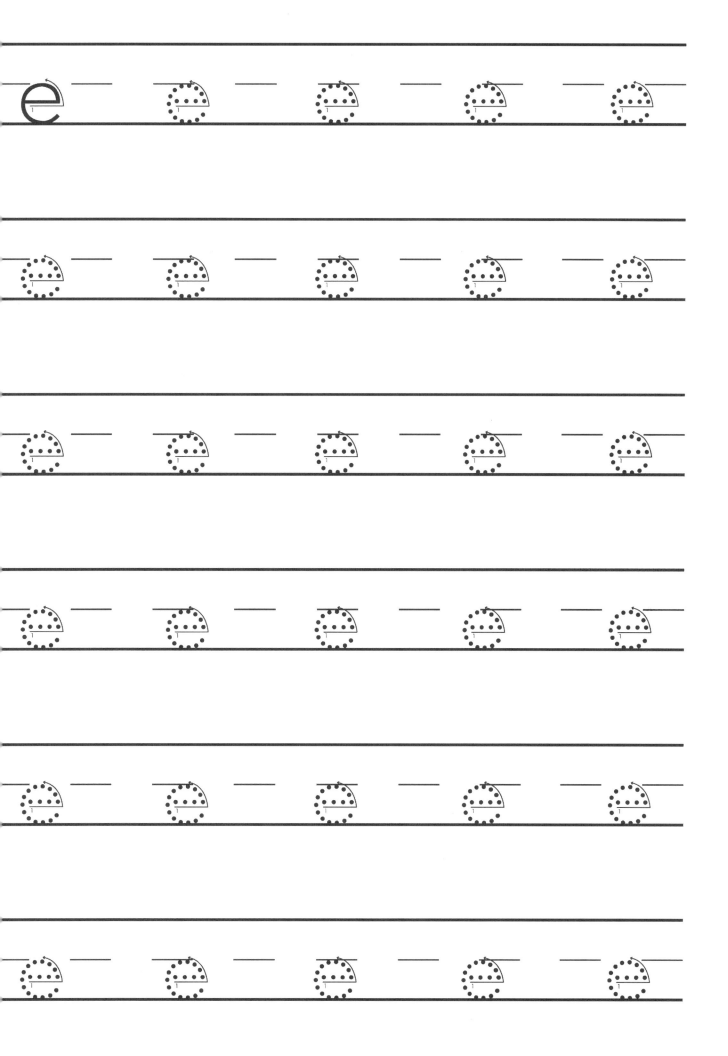

# The Latter F

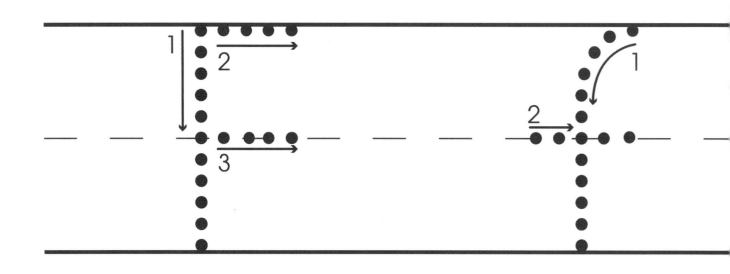

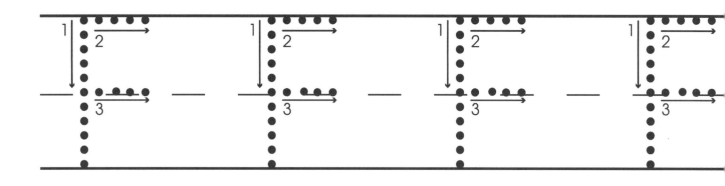

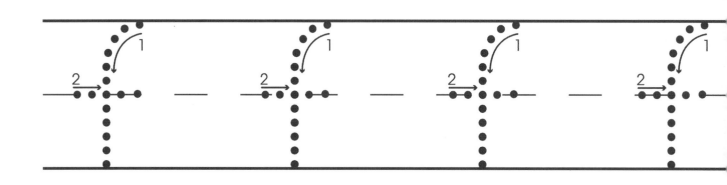

# F is for

F

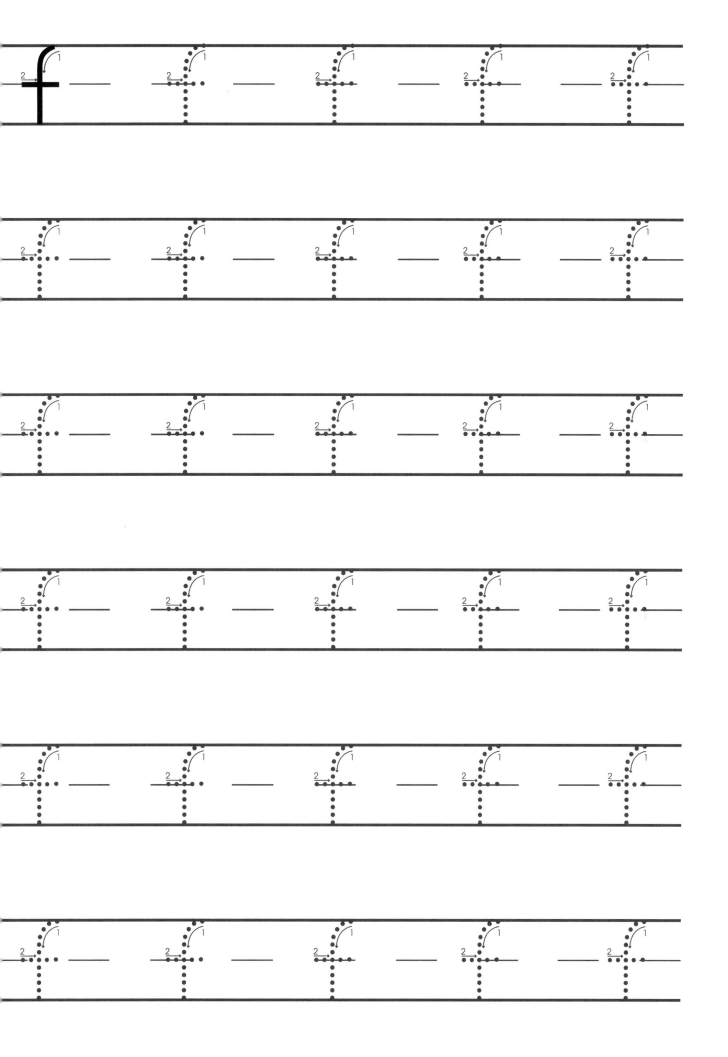

# The Latter G

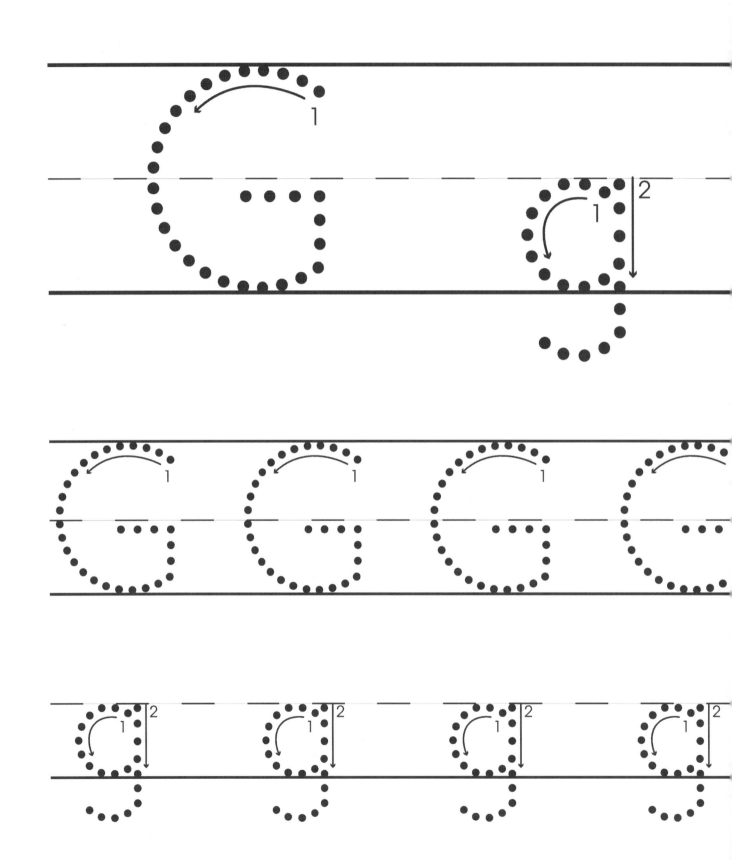

# G is for

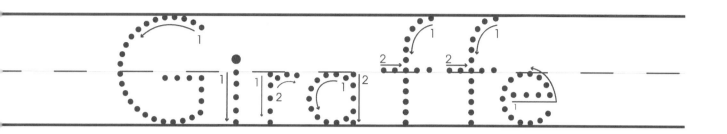

Giraffe

# G

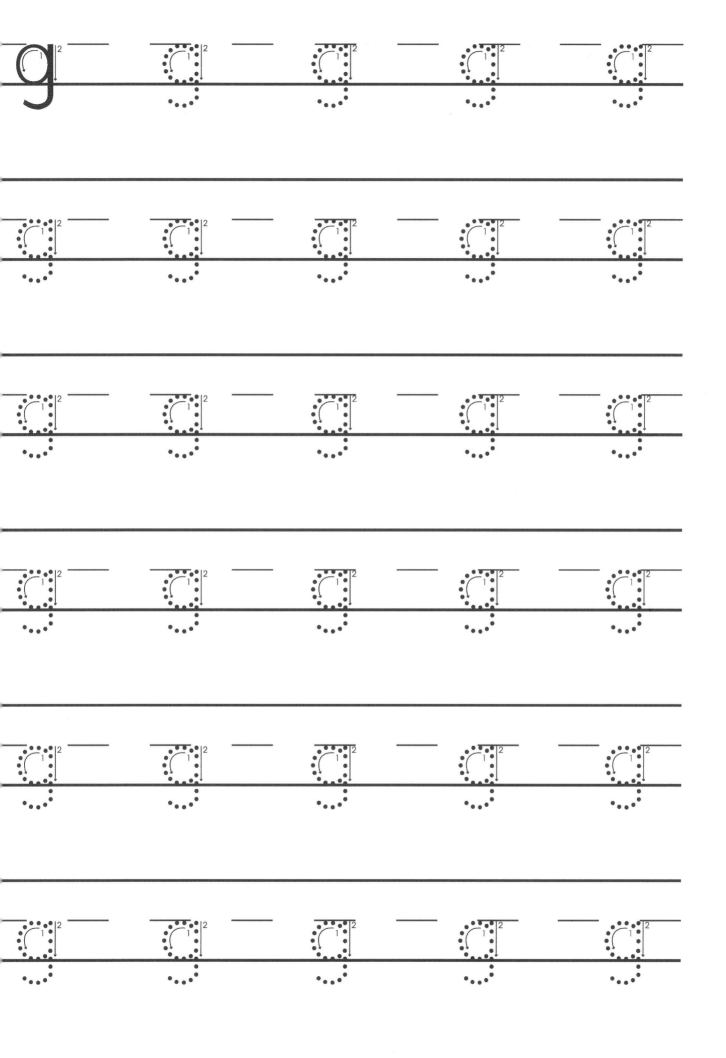

# The Latter H

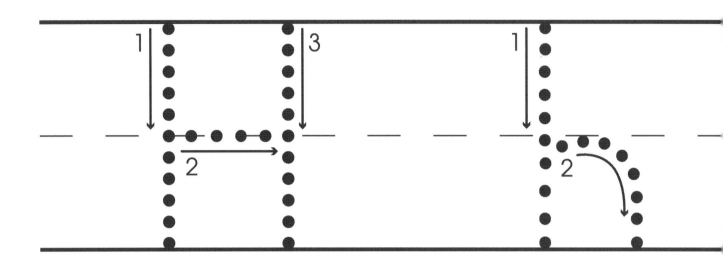

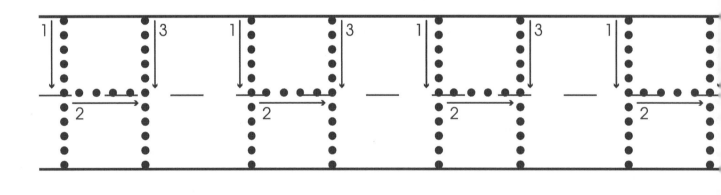

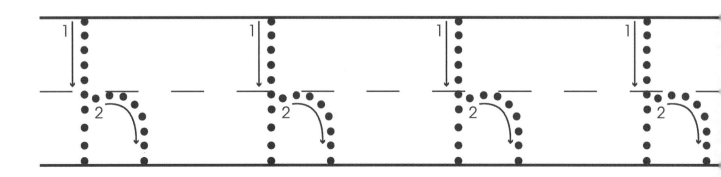

# H is for

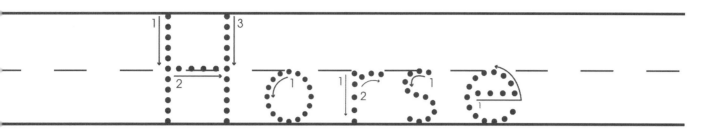

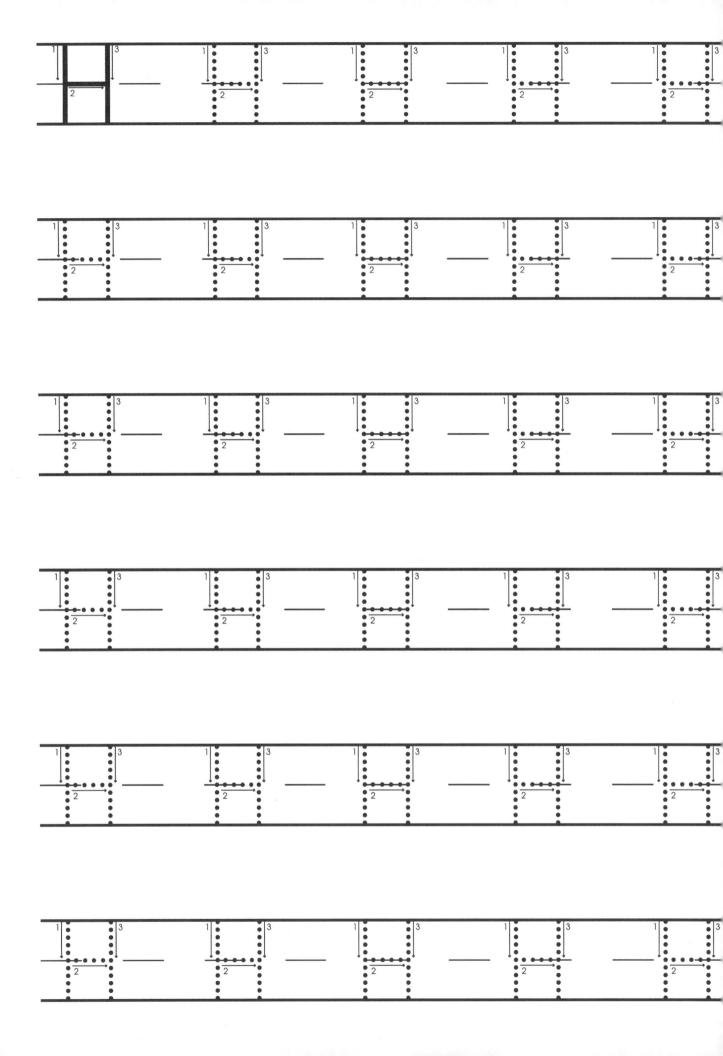

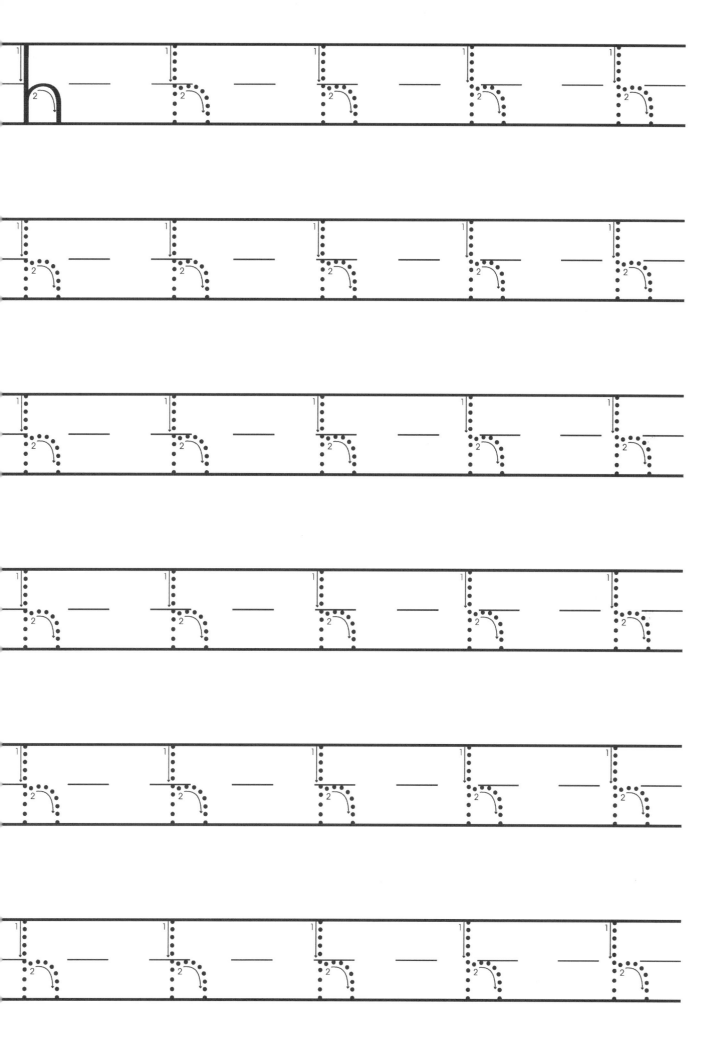

# The Latter I

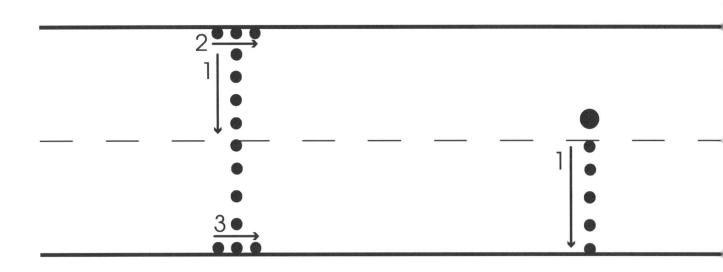

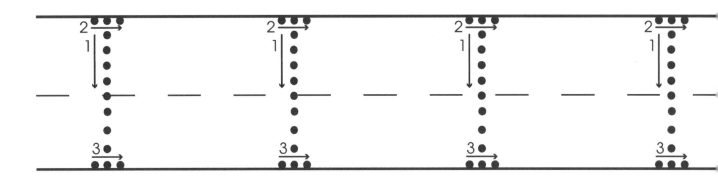

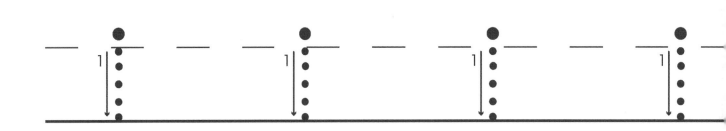

# I is for

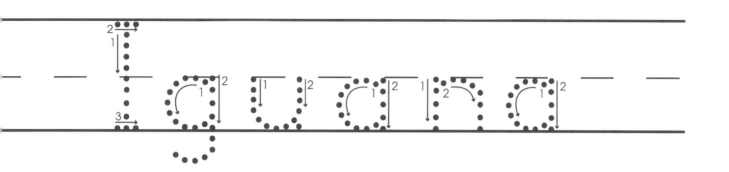

Iguana

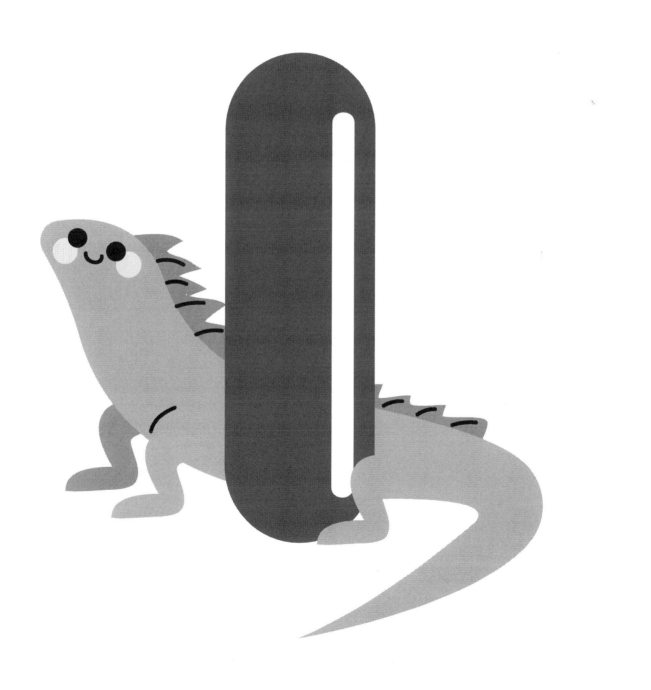

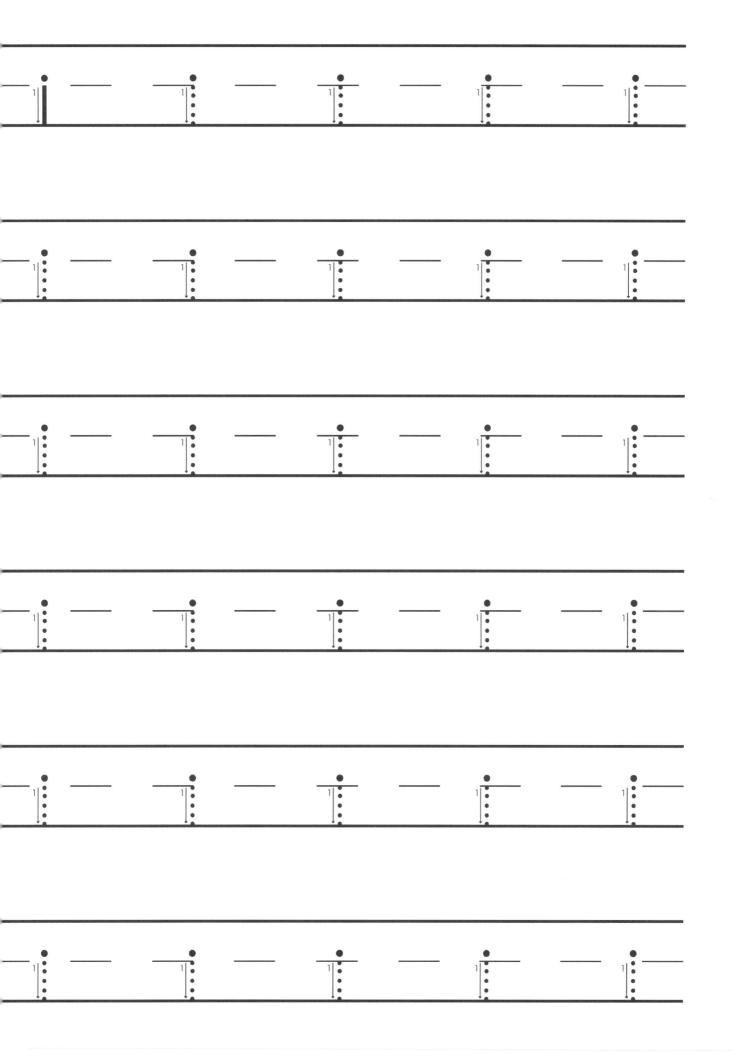

# The Latter J

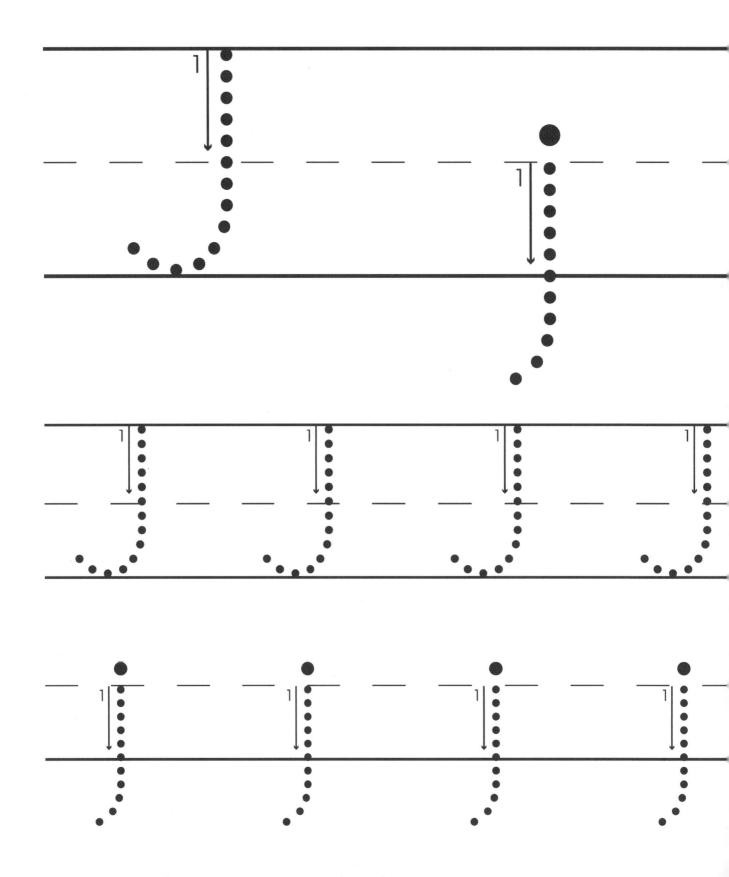

# J is for

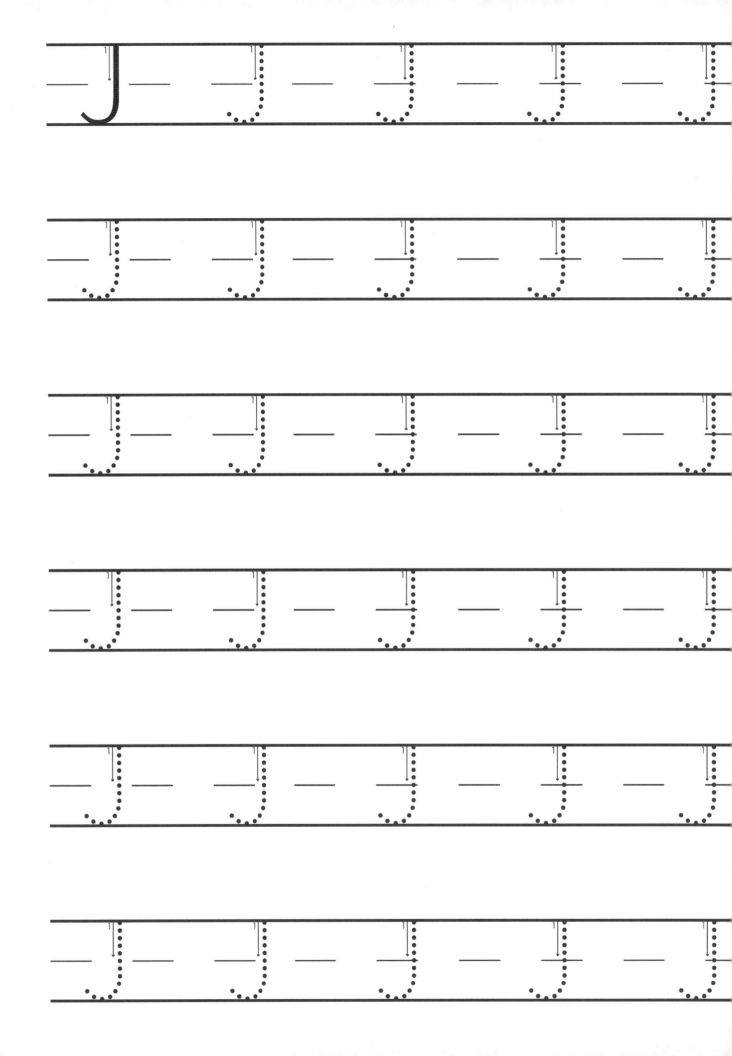

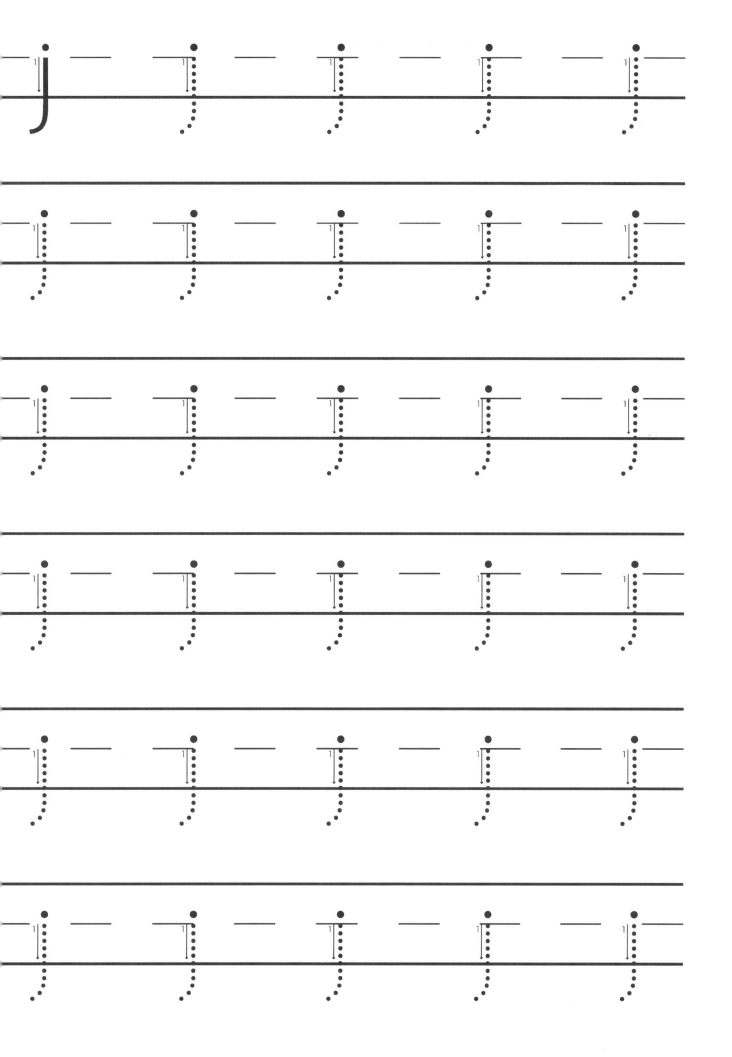

# The Latter K

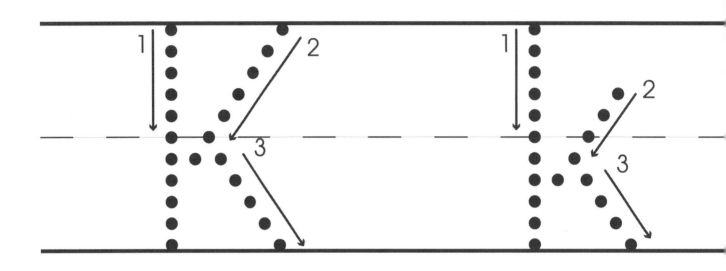

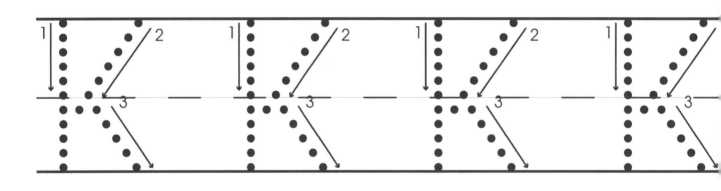

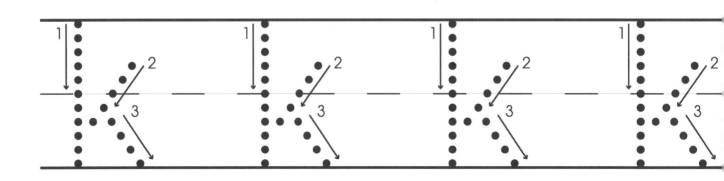

# K is for

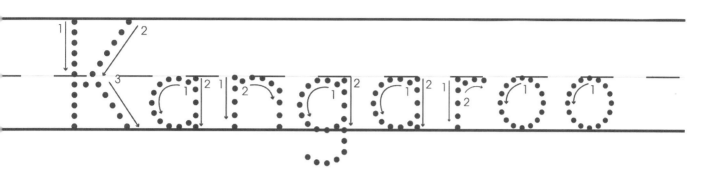

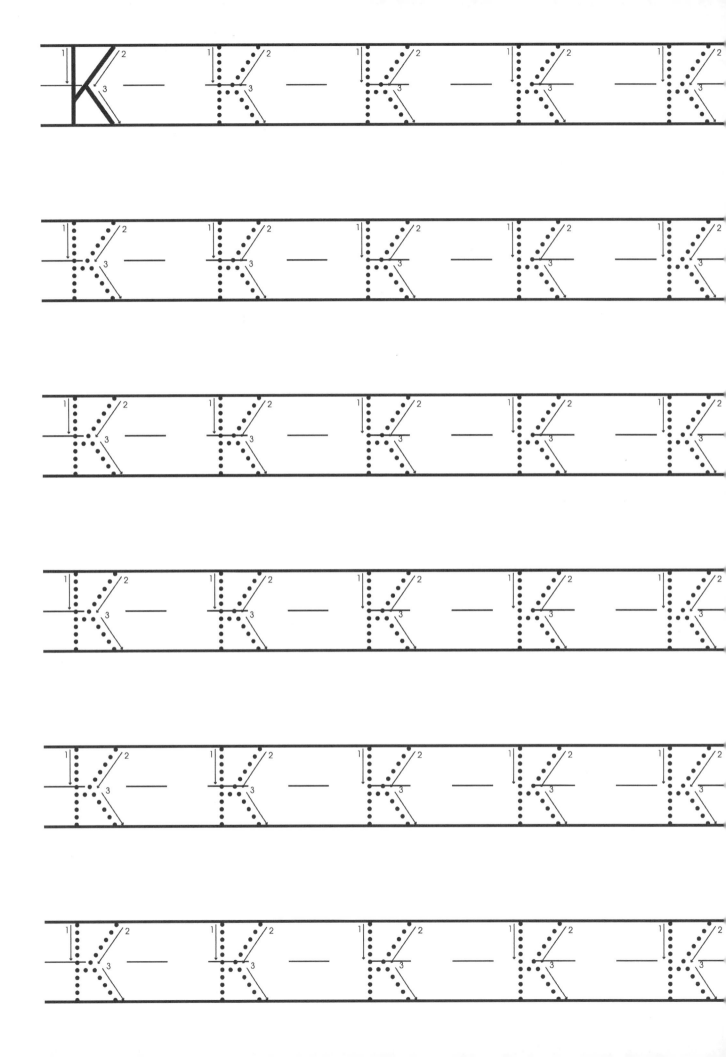

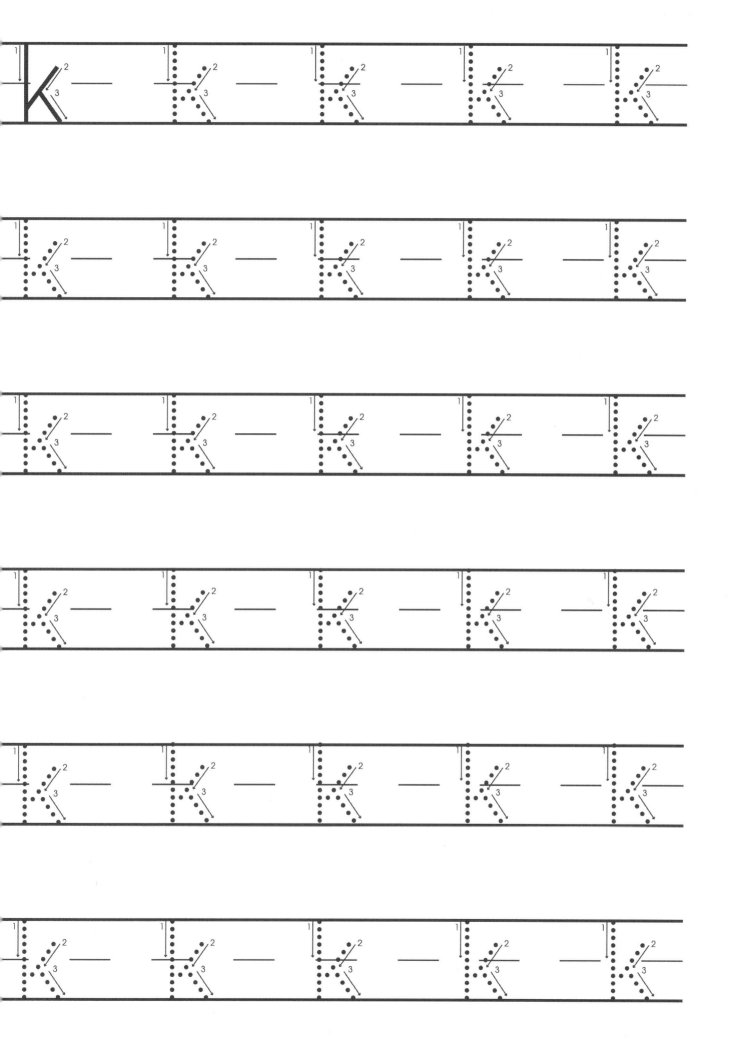

# The Latter L

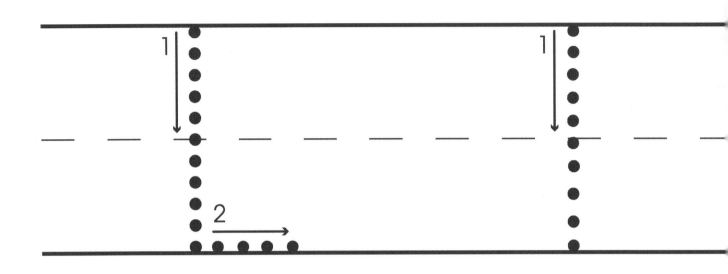

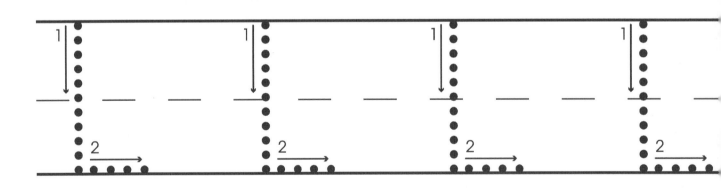

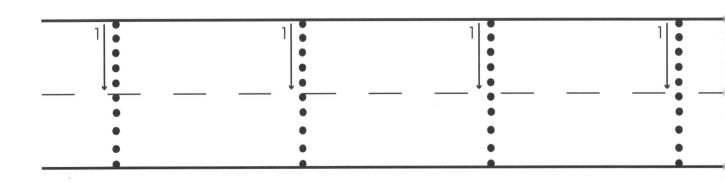

# L is for

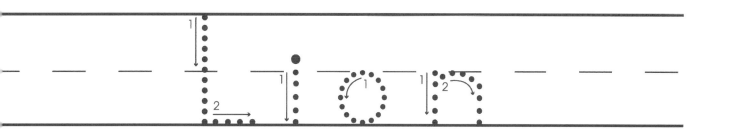

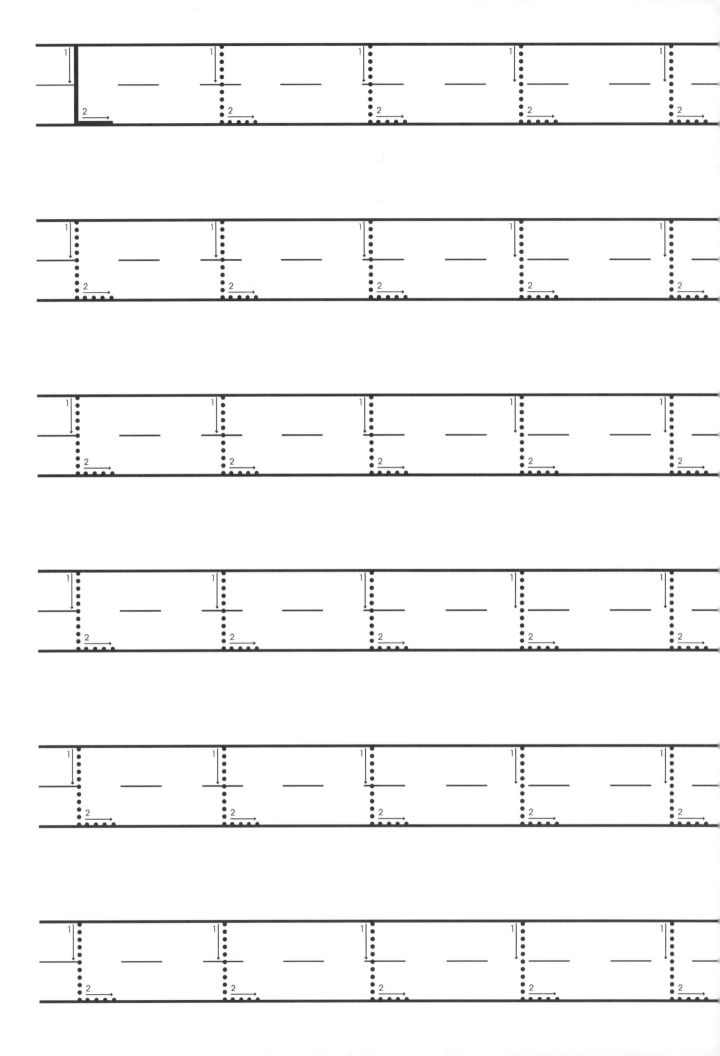

# The Latter M

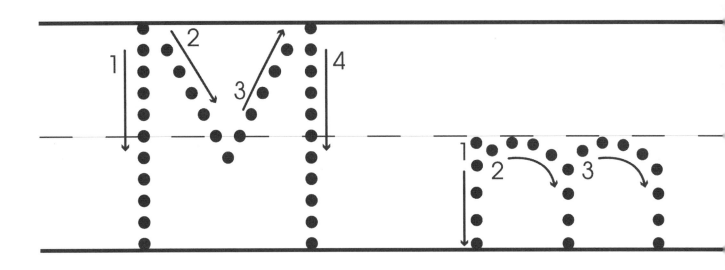

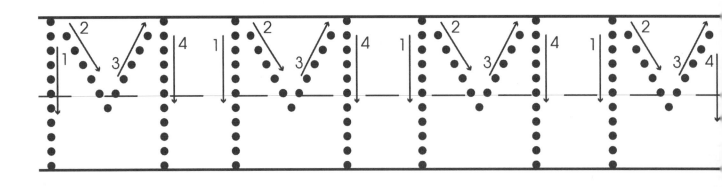

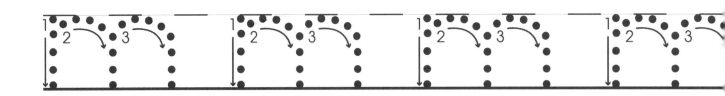

# M is for

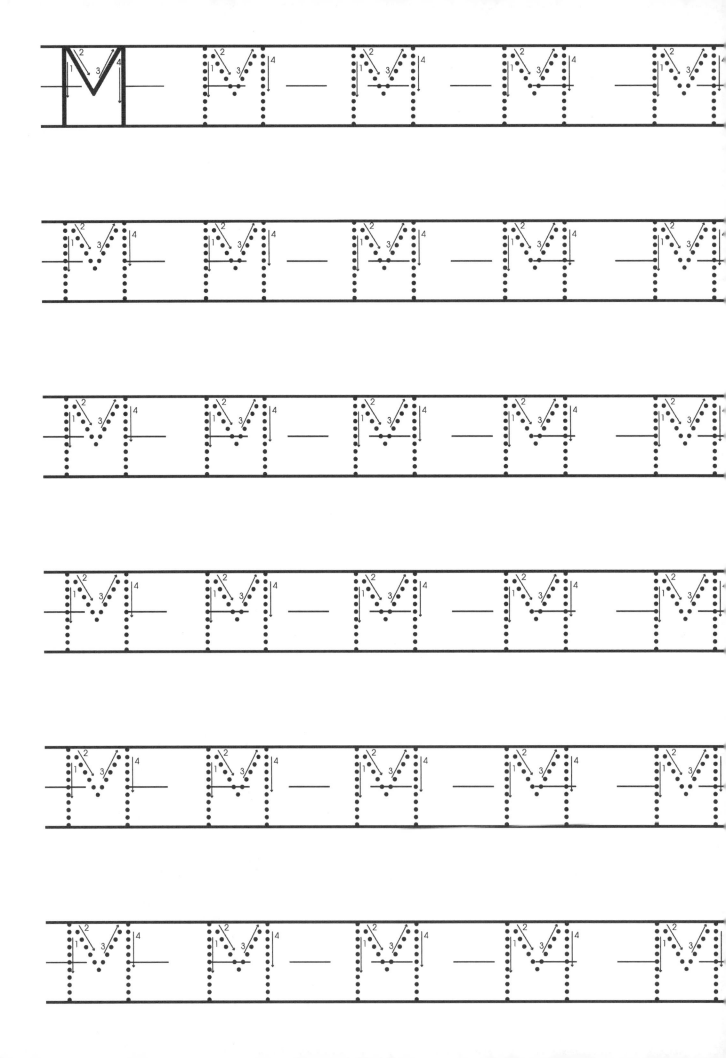

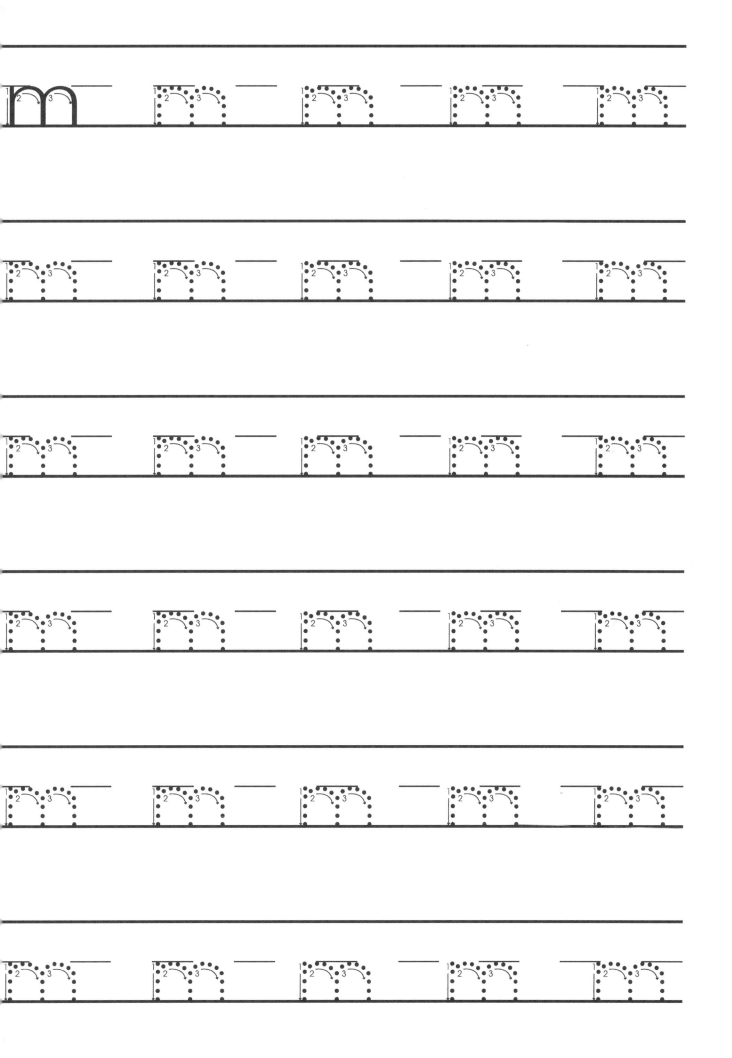

# The Latter N

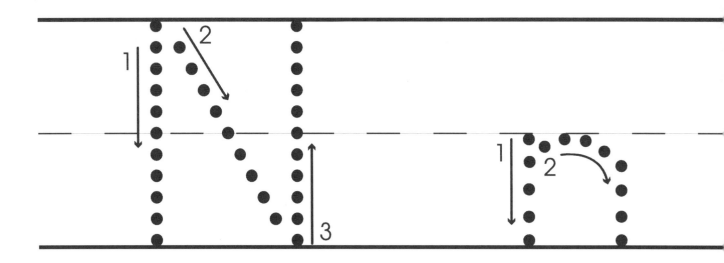

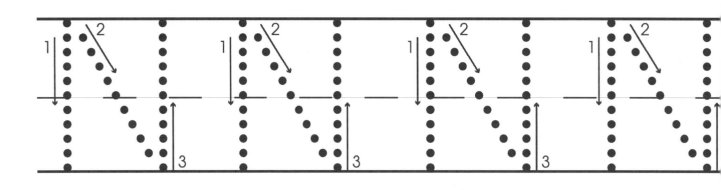

# N is for

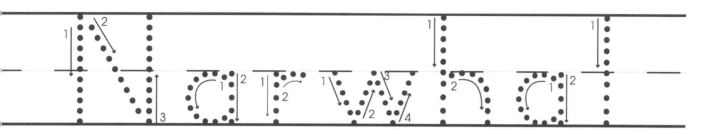

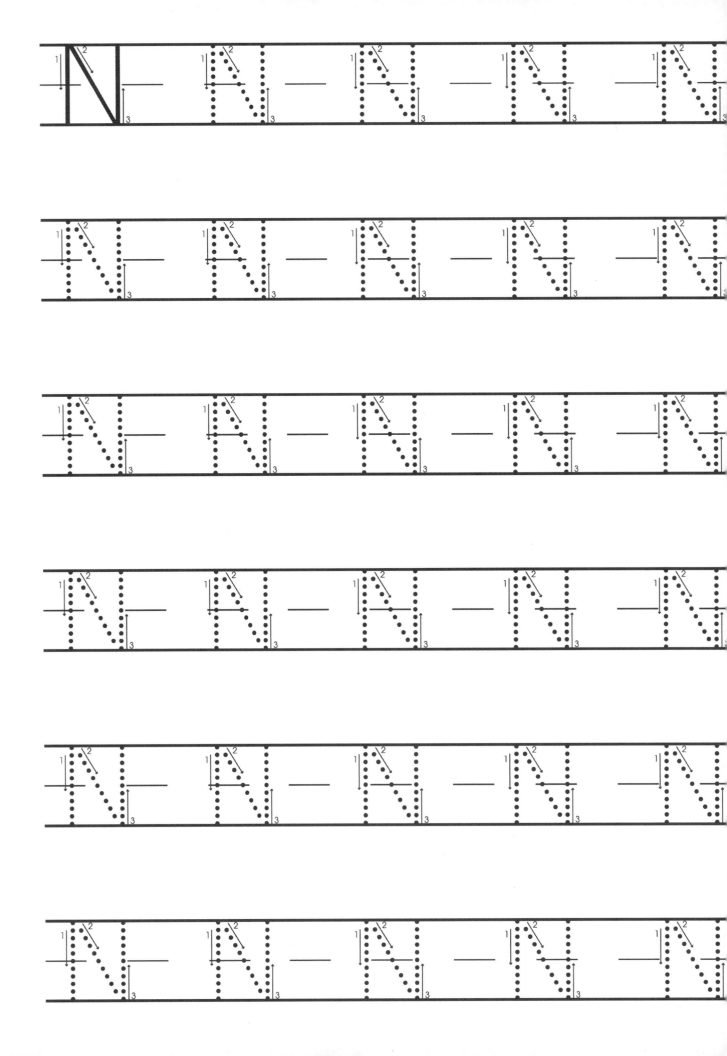

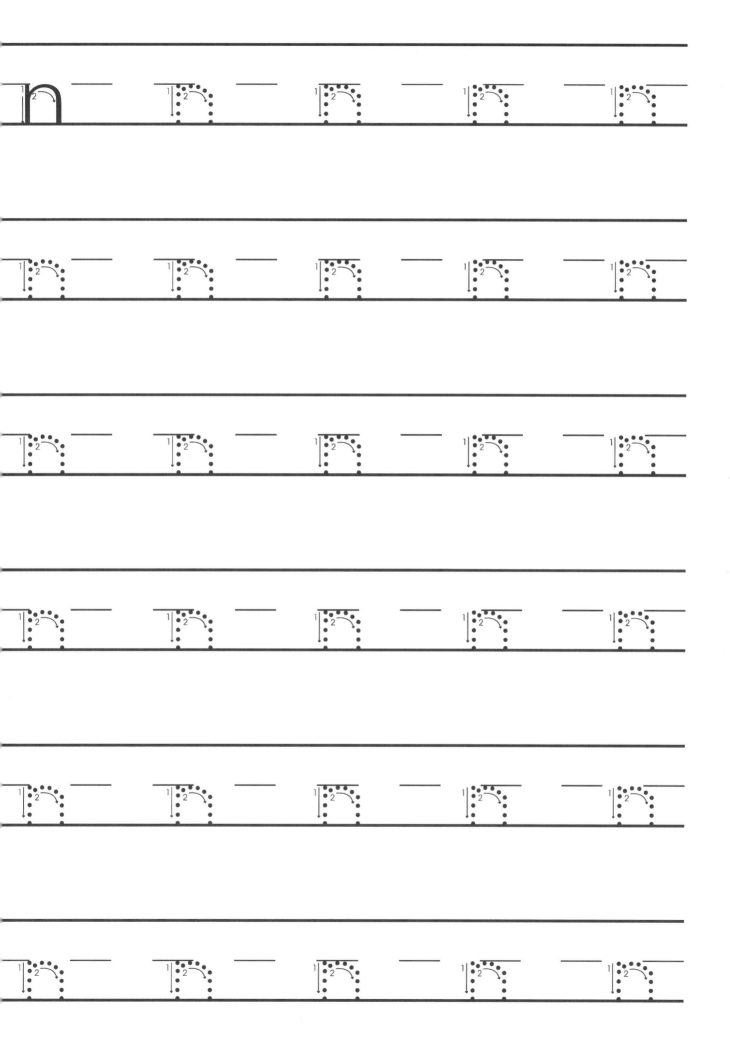

# The Latter O

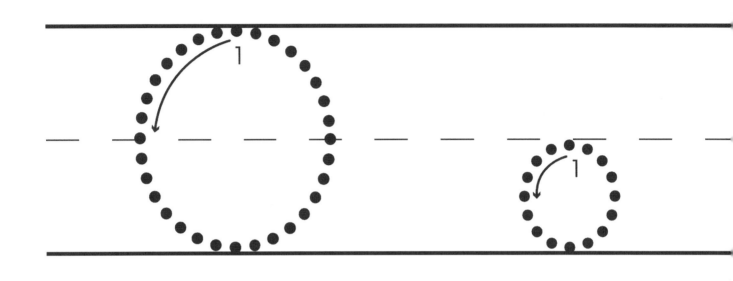

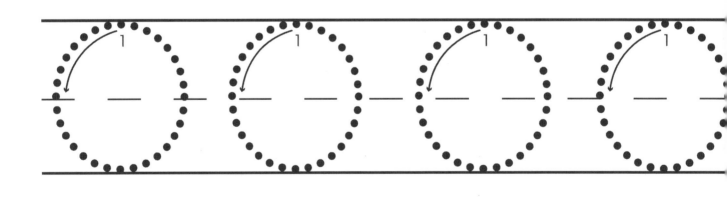

# O is for

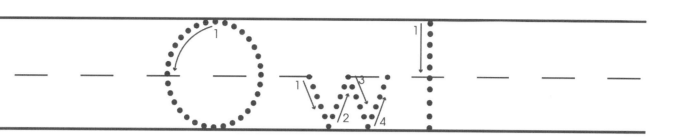

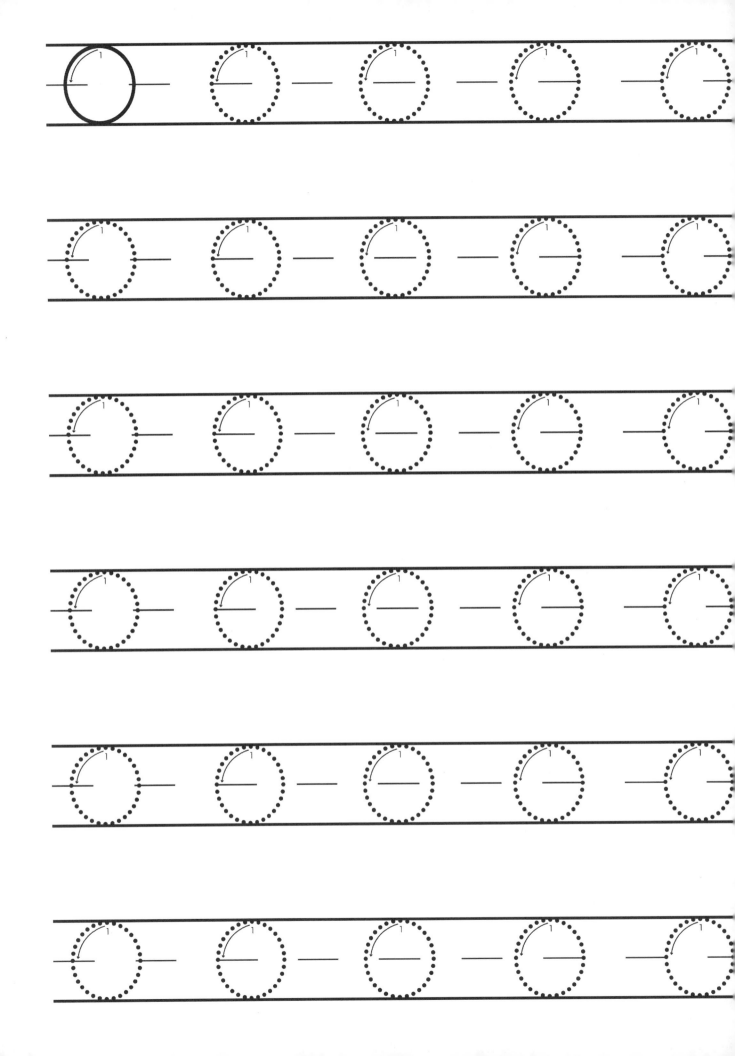

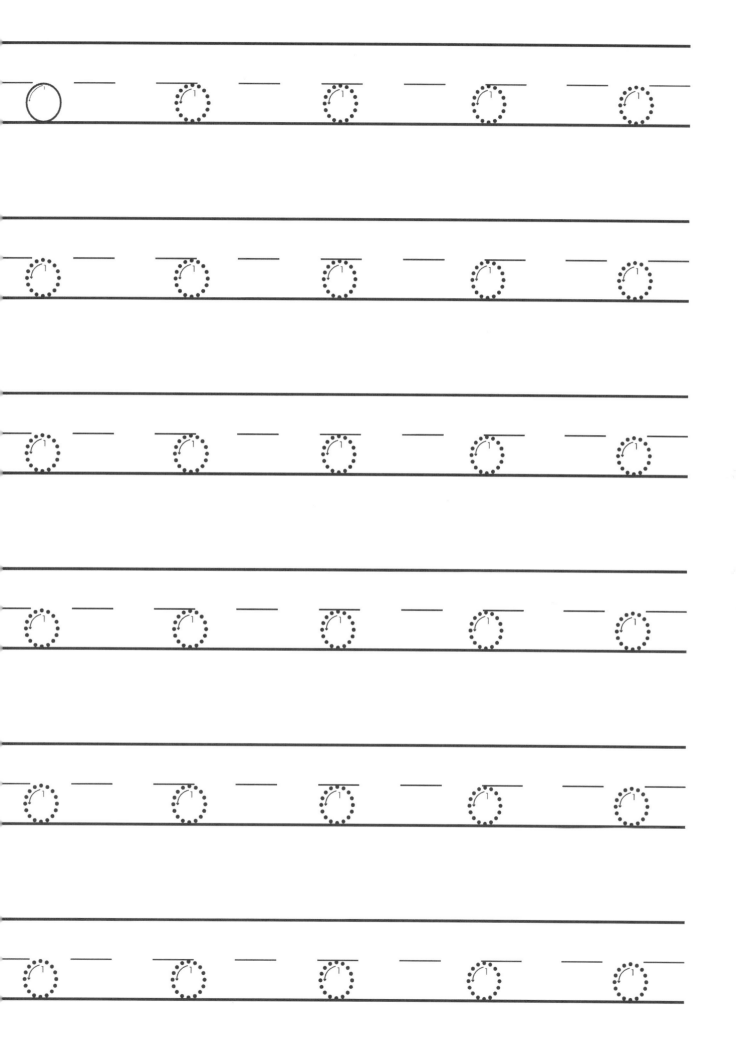

# The Latter P

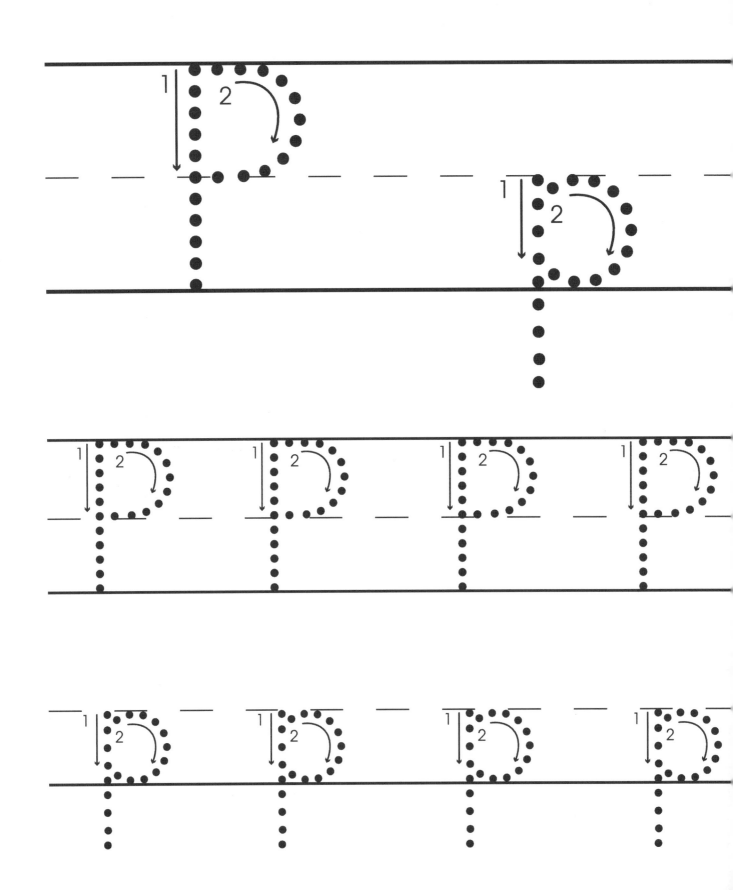

# P is for

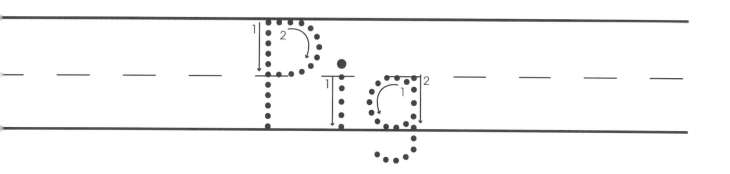

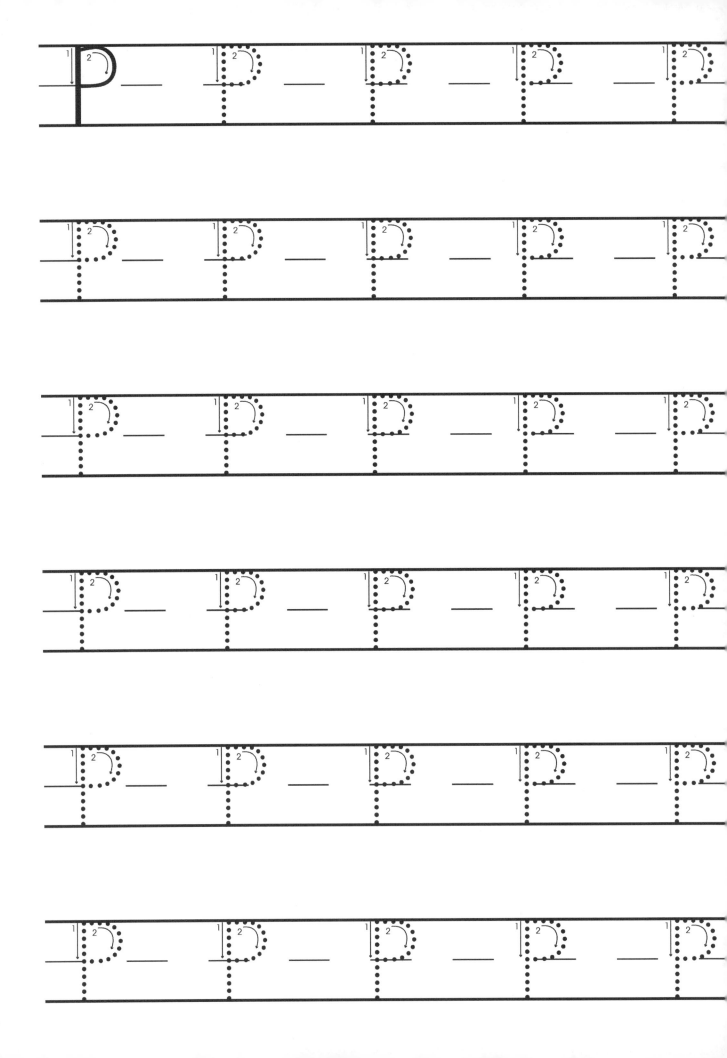

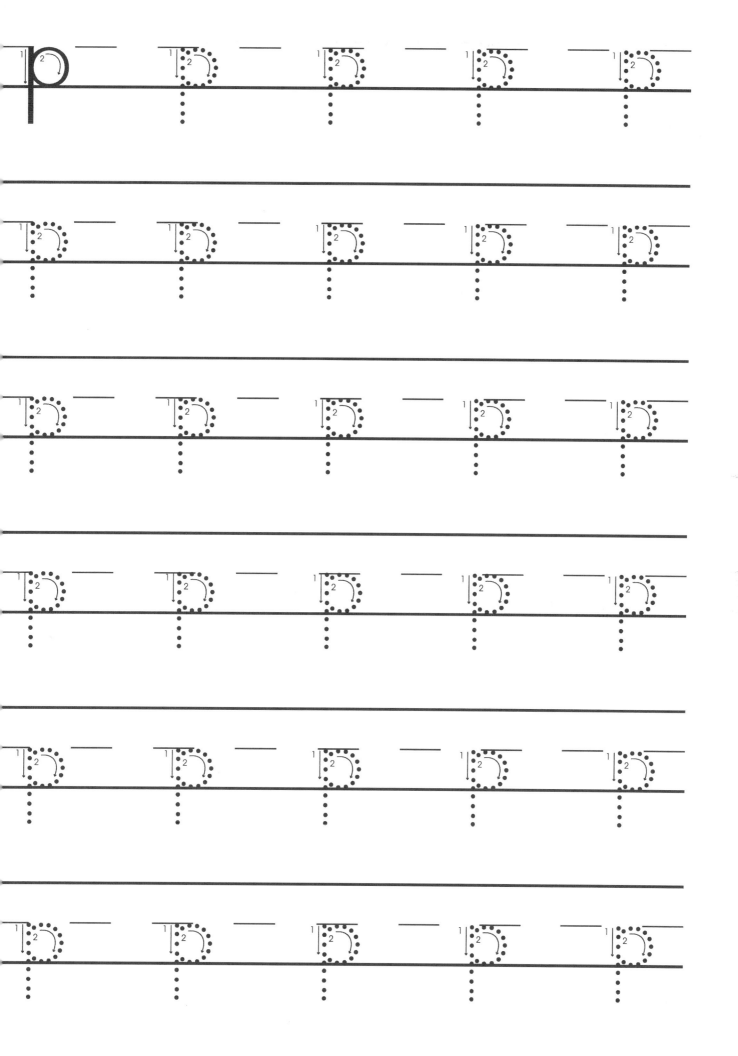

# The Latter Q

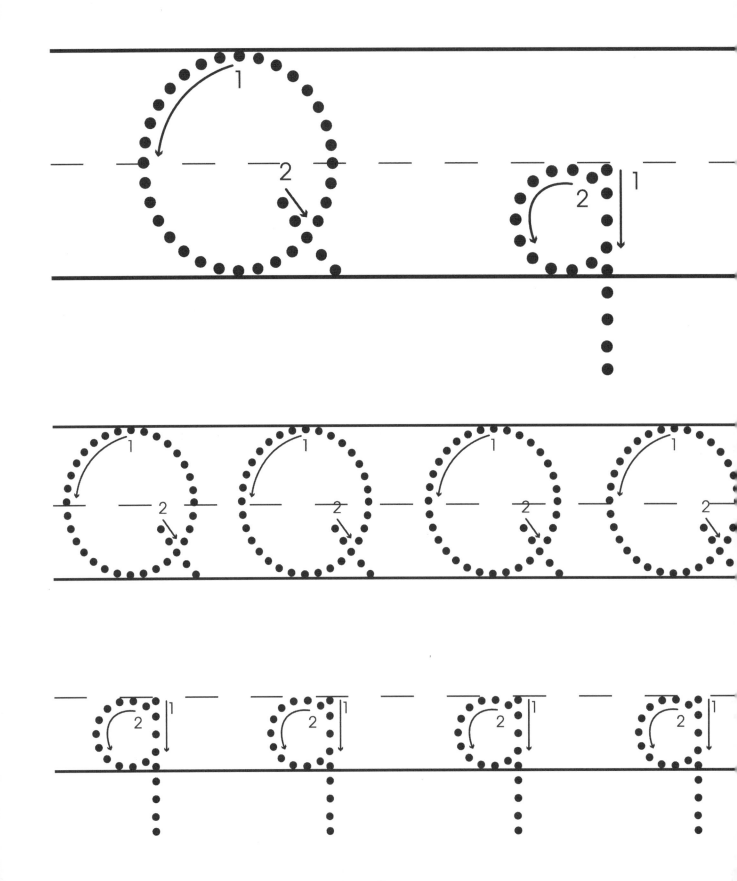

# Q is for

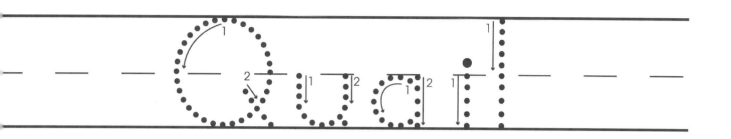

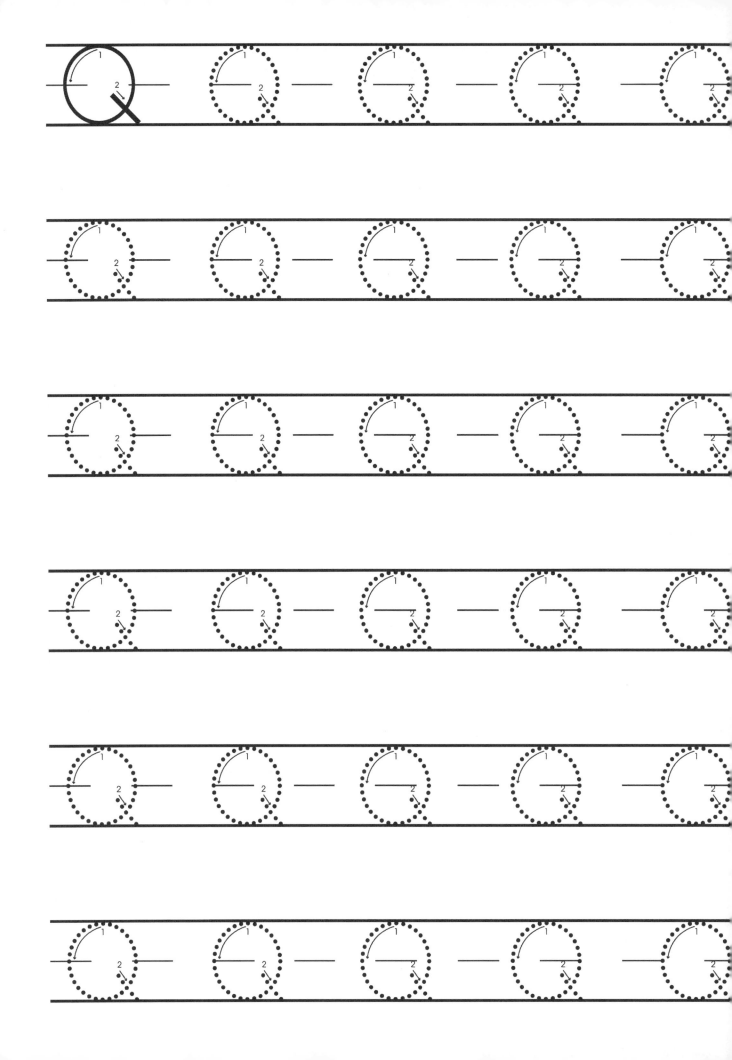

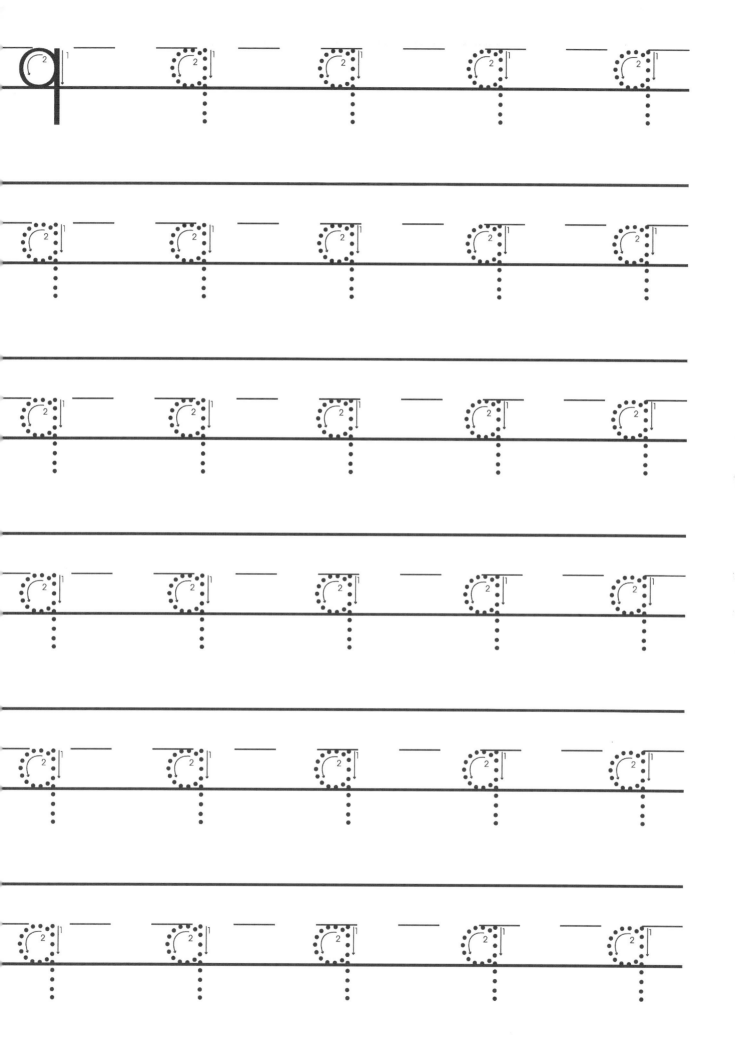

# The Latter R

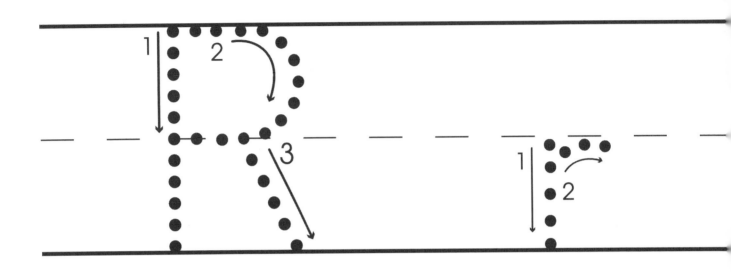

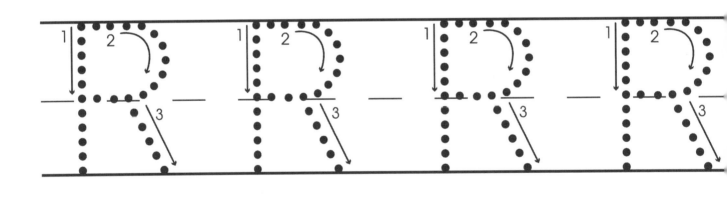

# R is for

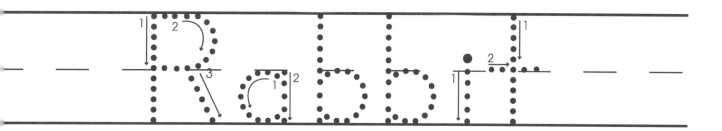

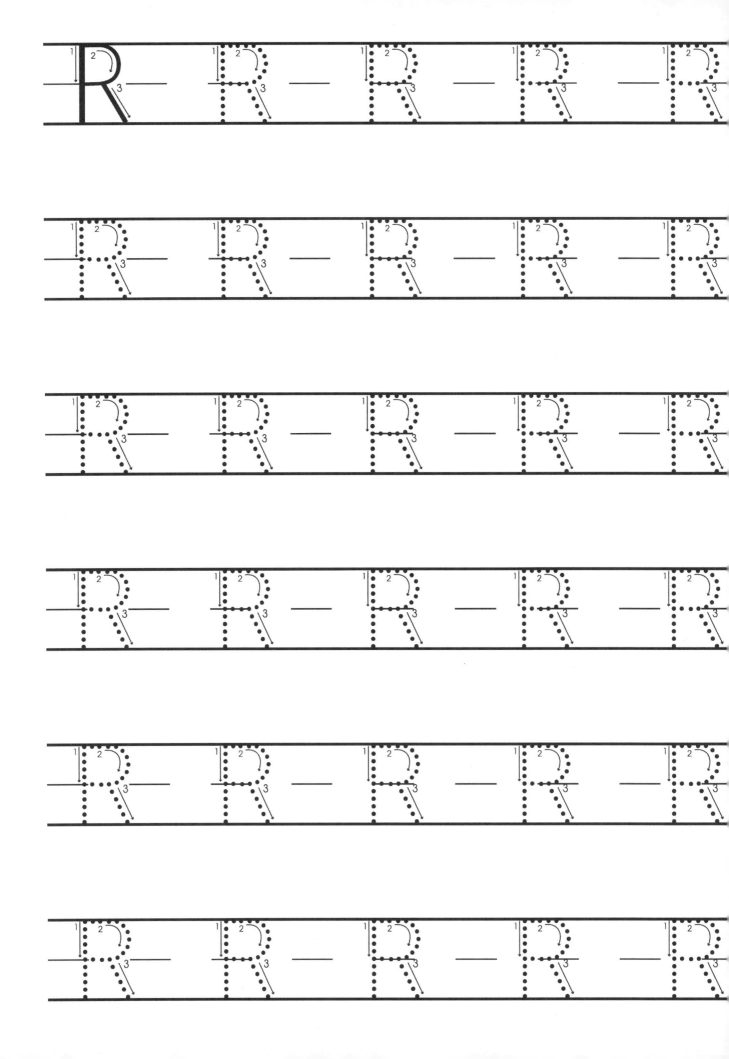

r

# The Latter S

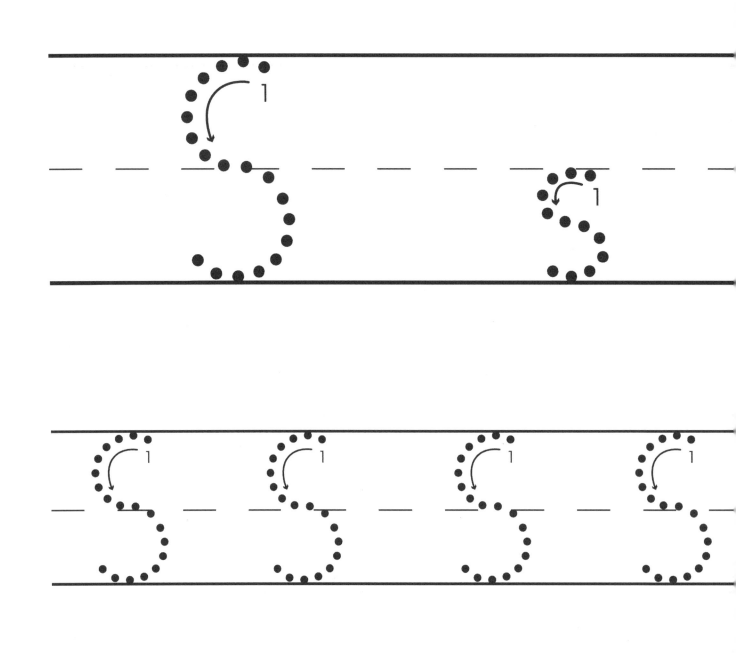

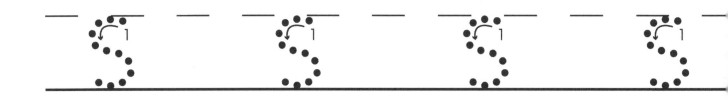

# S is for

Scorpion

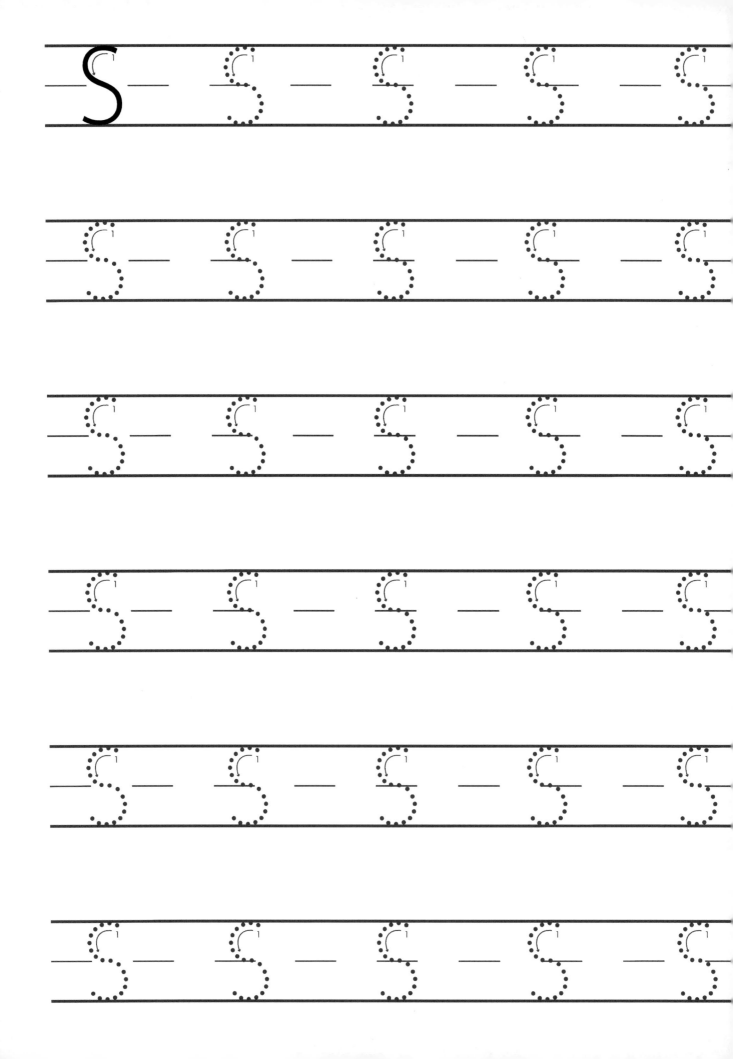

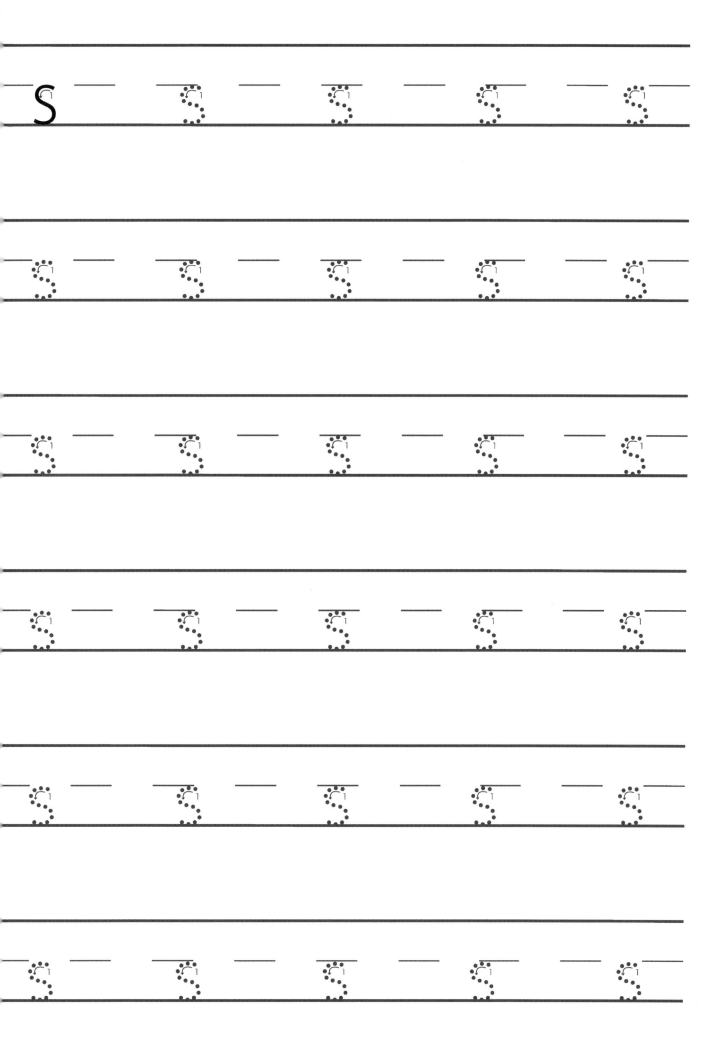

# The Latter T

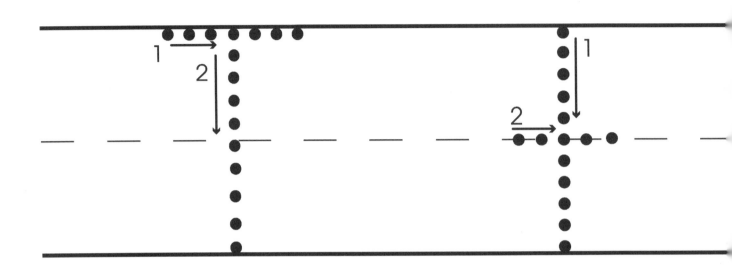

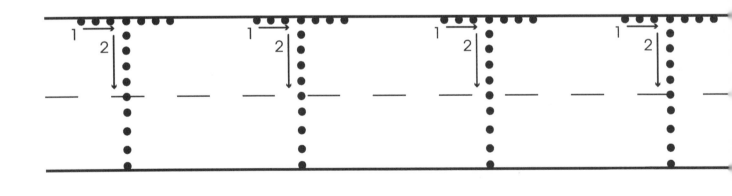

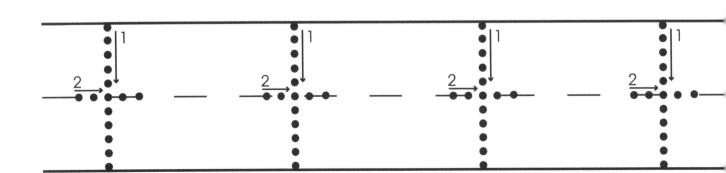

# T is for

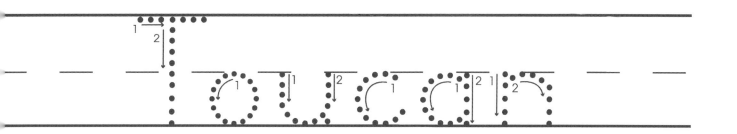

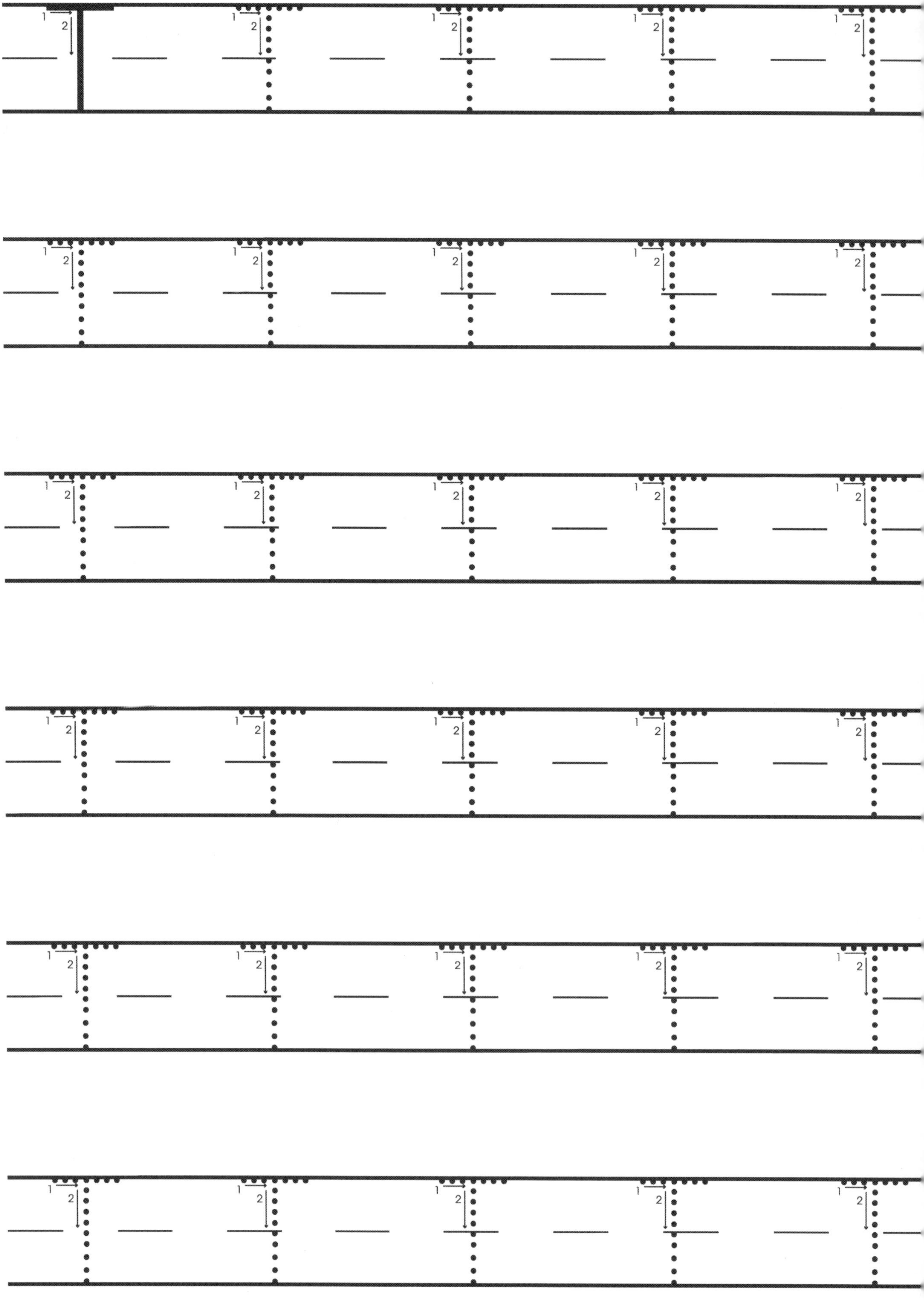

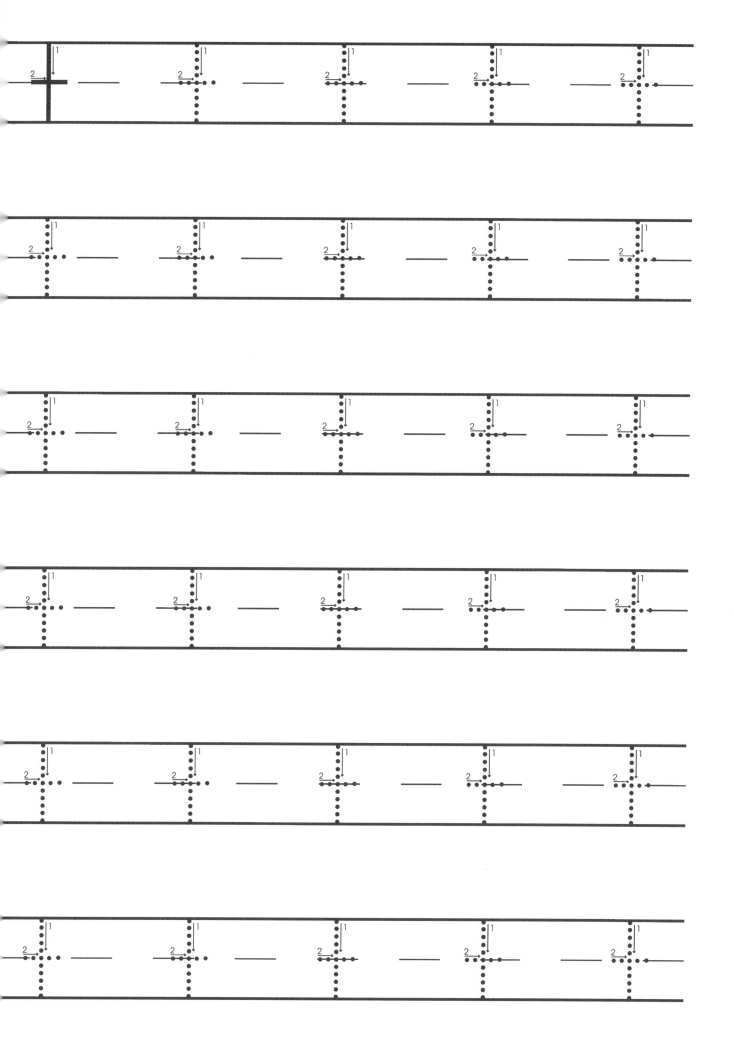

# The Latter U

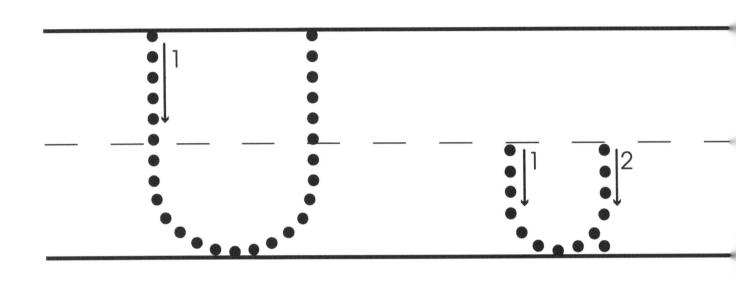

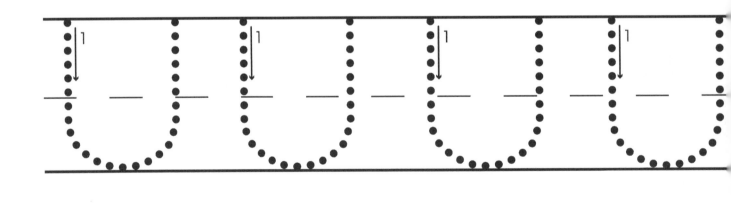

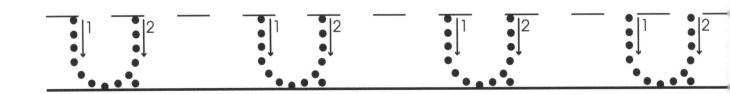

# U is for

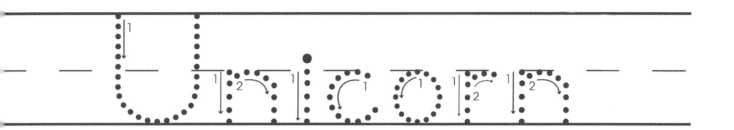

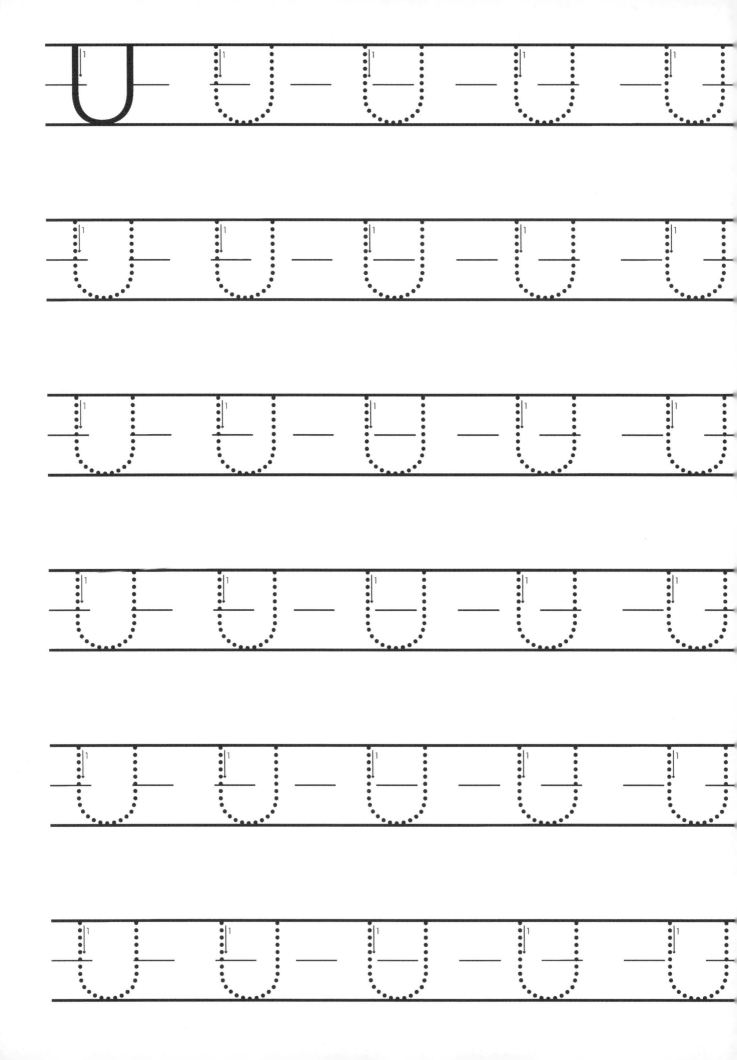

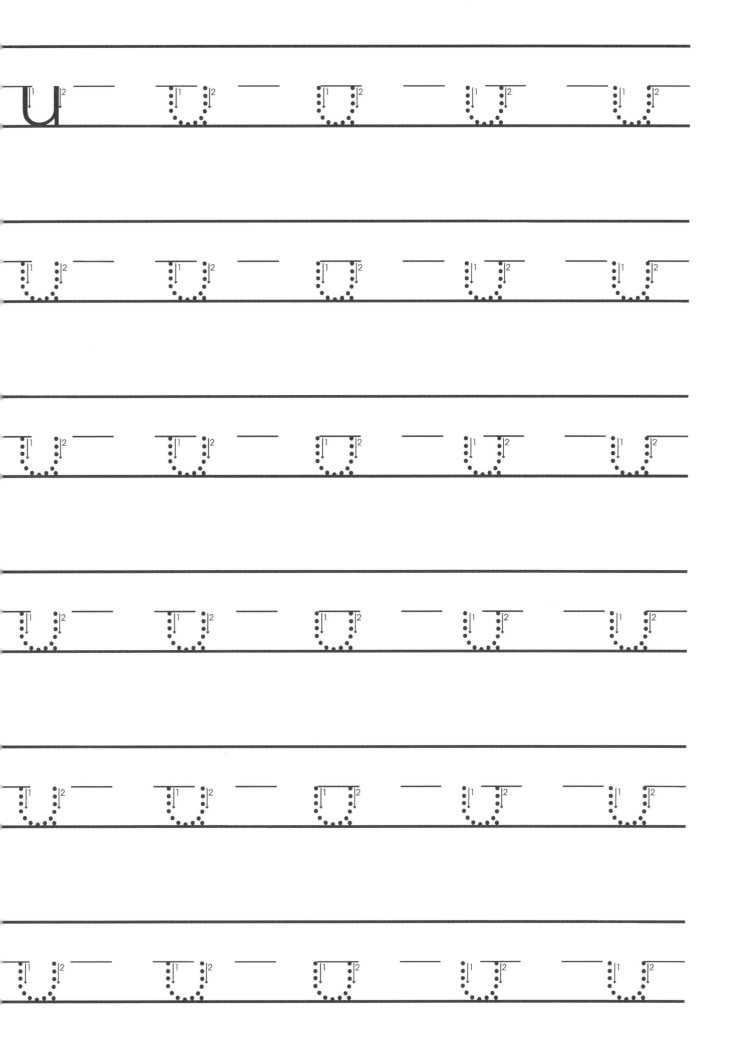

# The Latter V

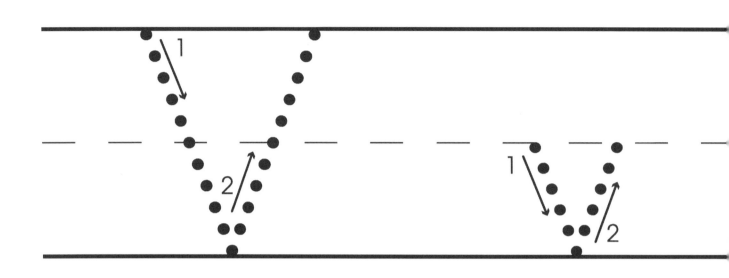

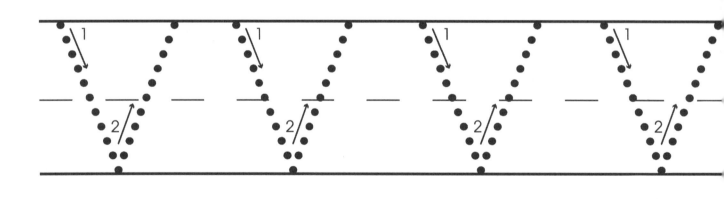

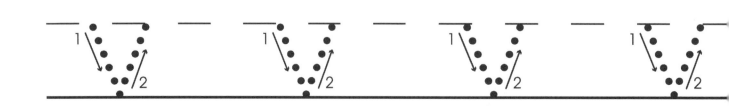

# V is for

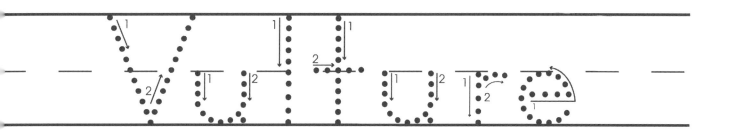

Vulture

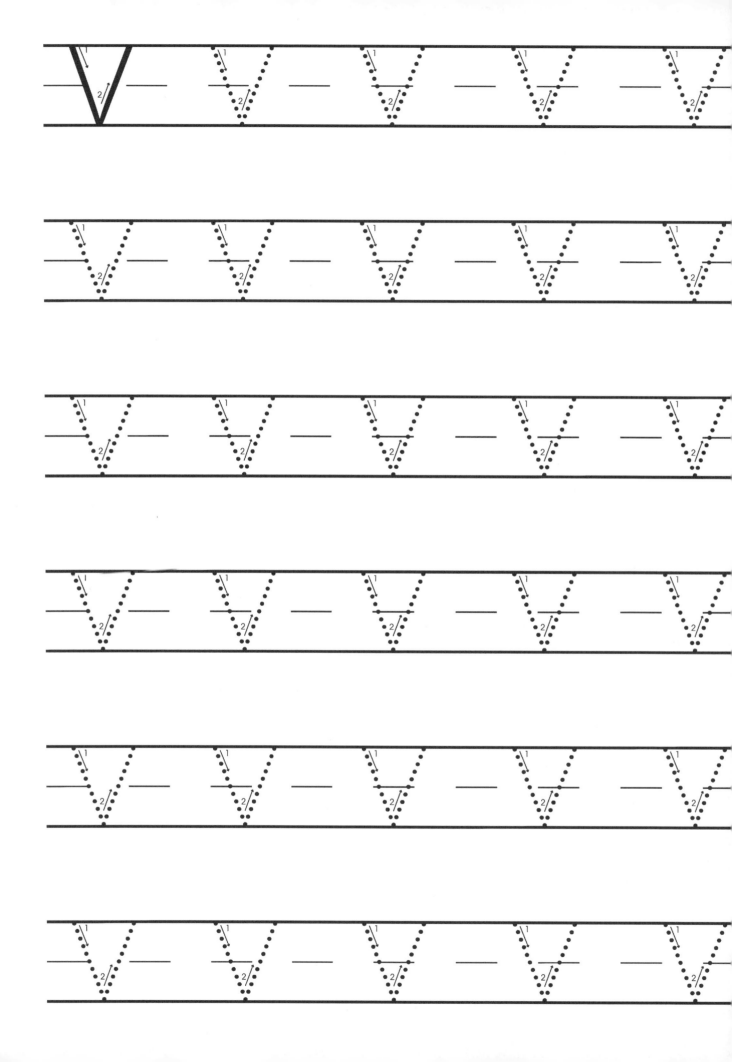

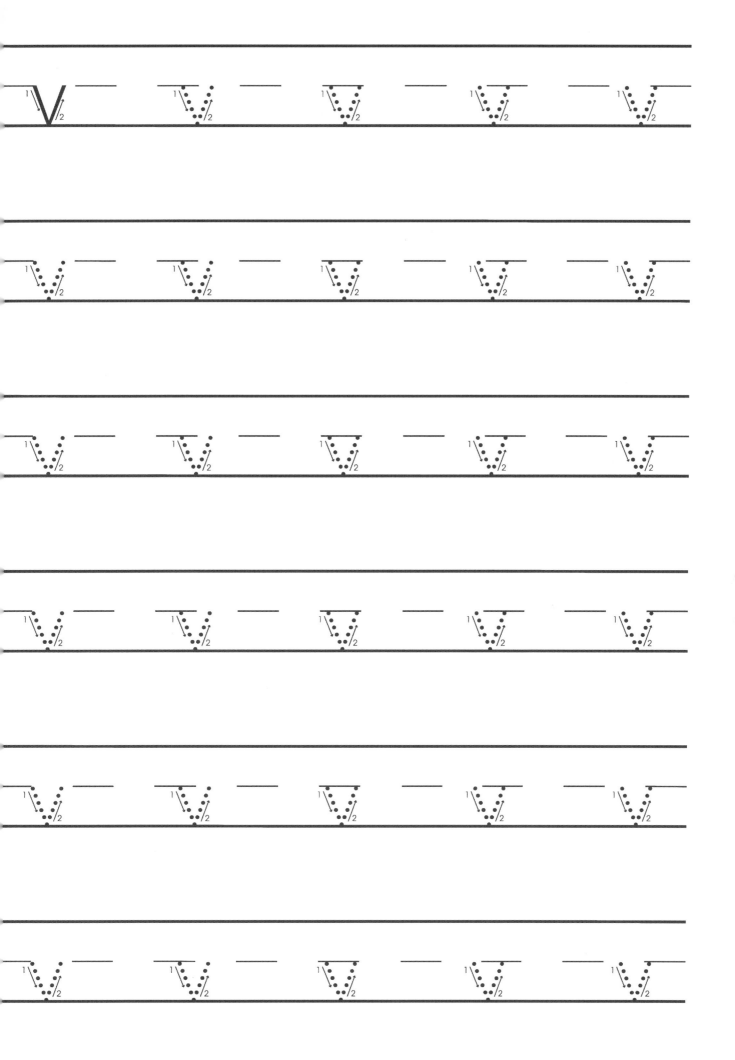

# The Latter W

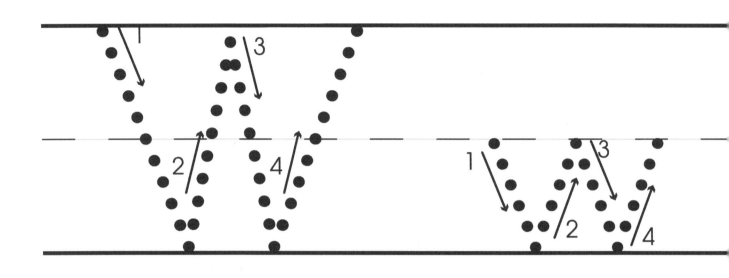

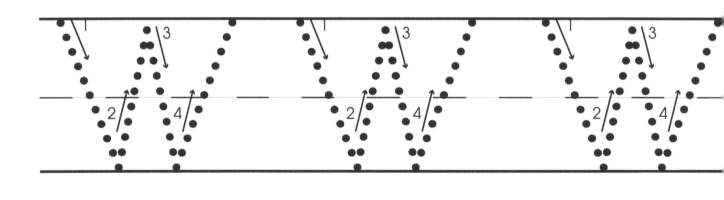

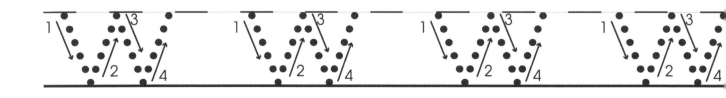

# W is for

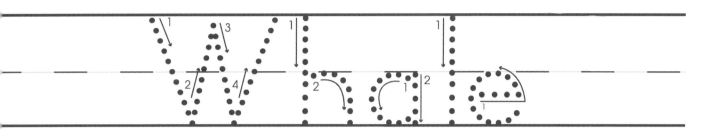

Whale

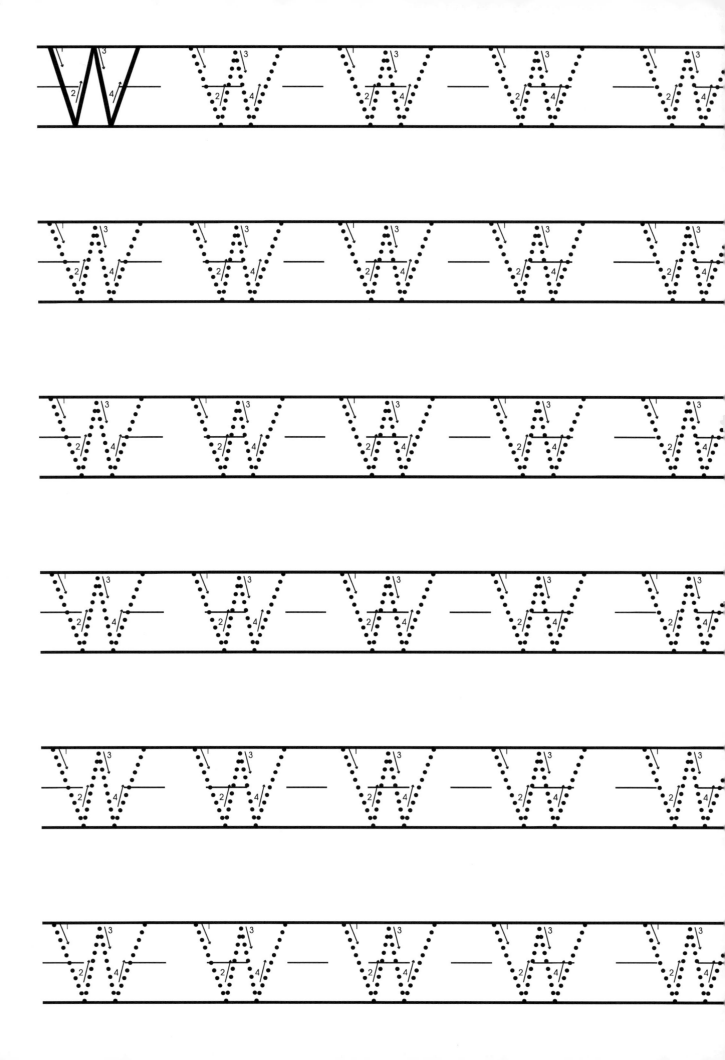

# The Latter X

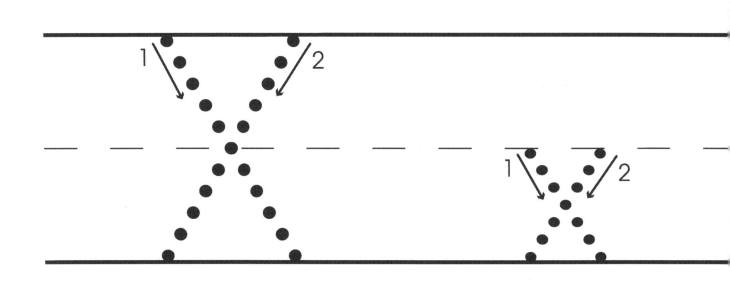

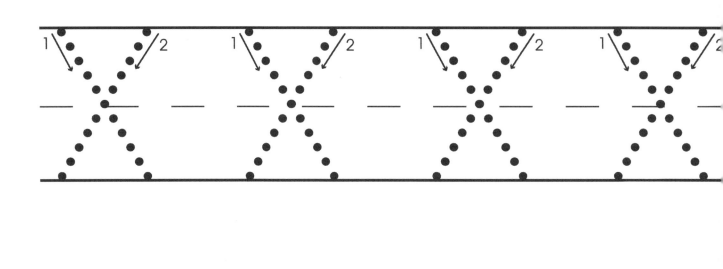

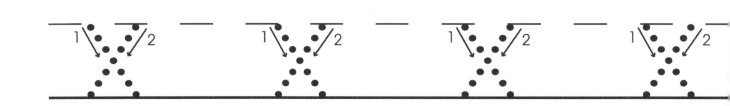

# X is for

X-Ray Fish

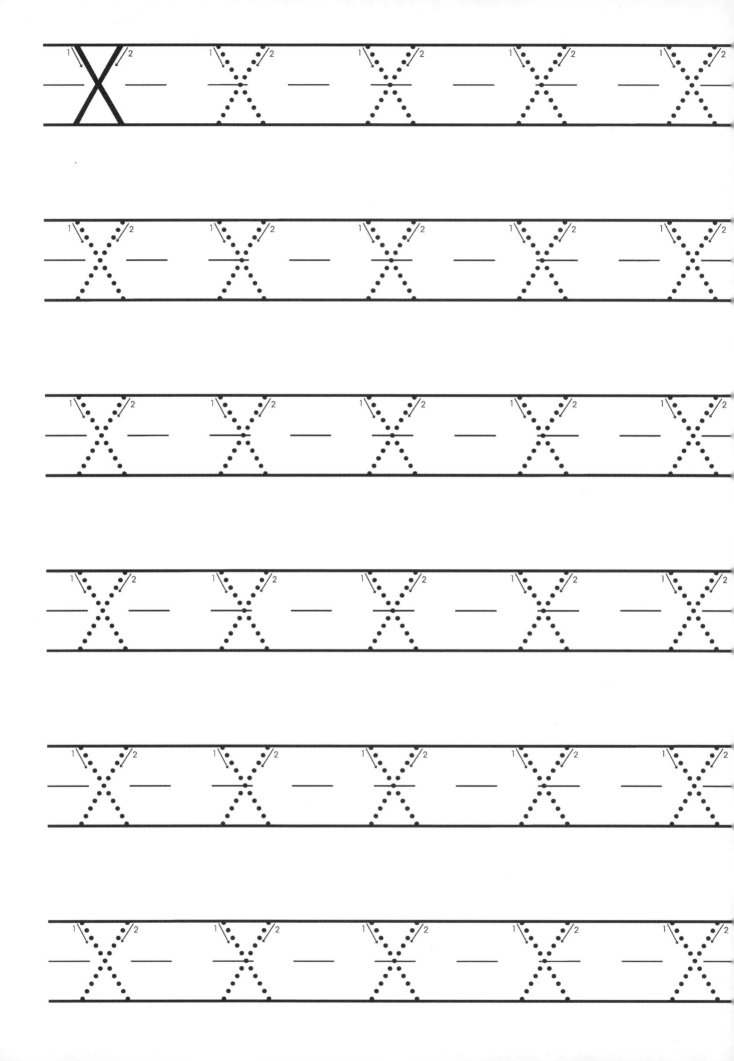

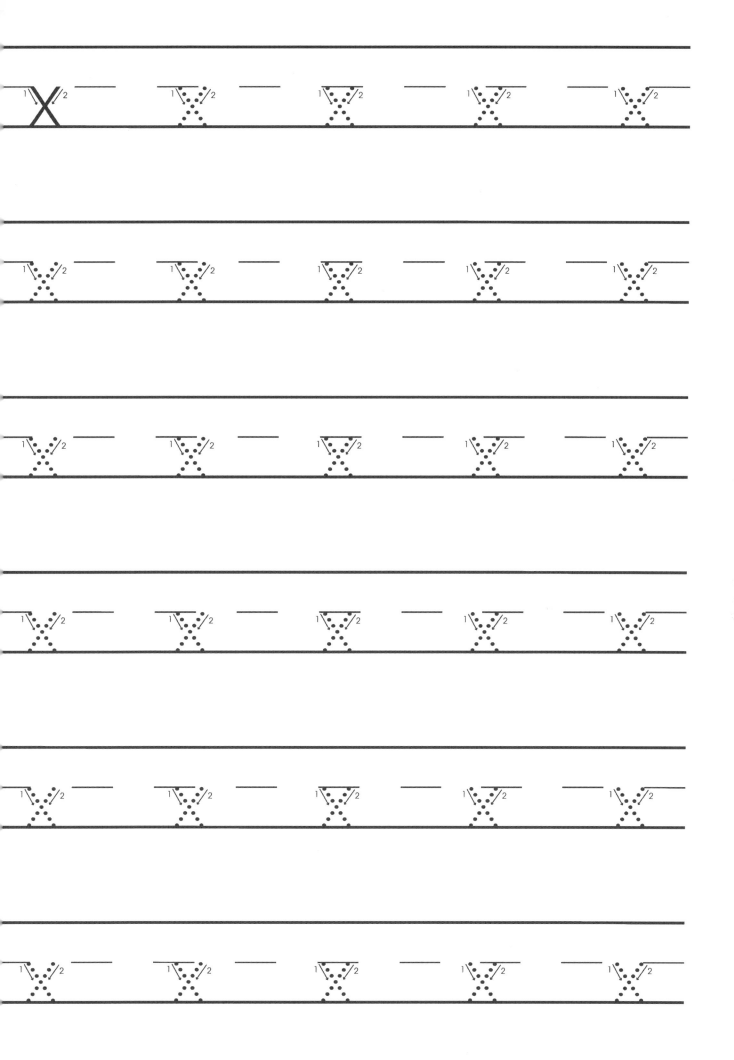

# The Latter Y

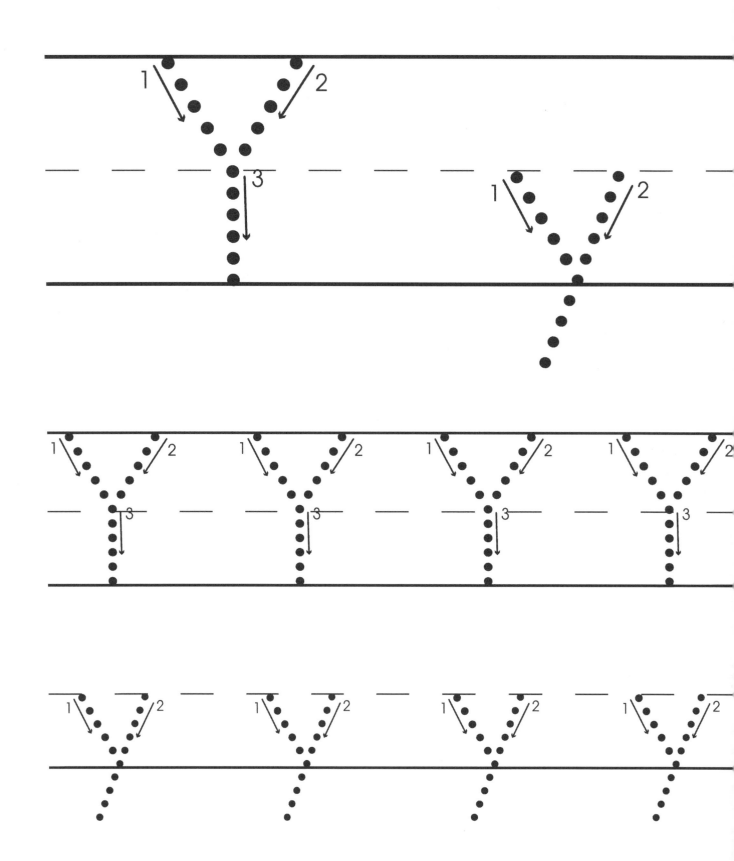

# Y is for

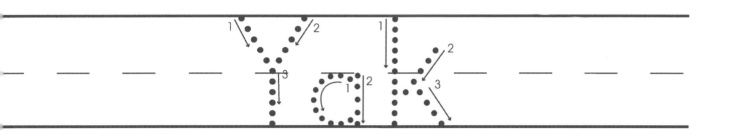

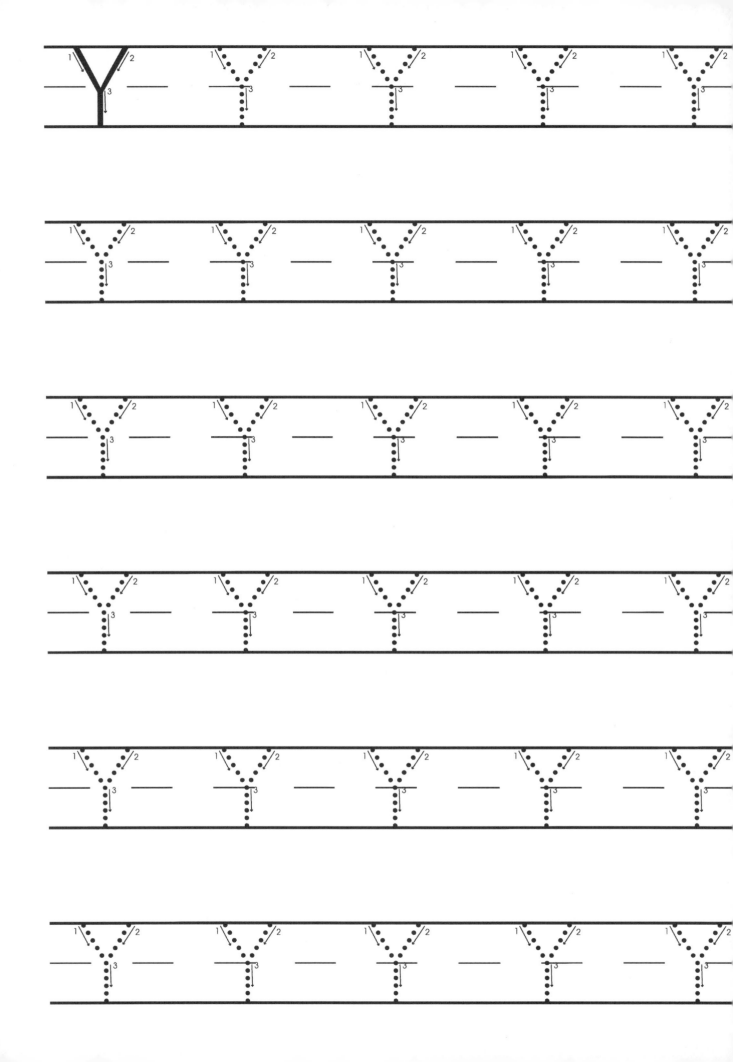

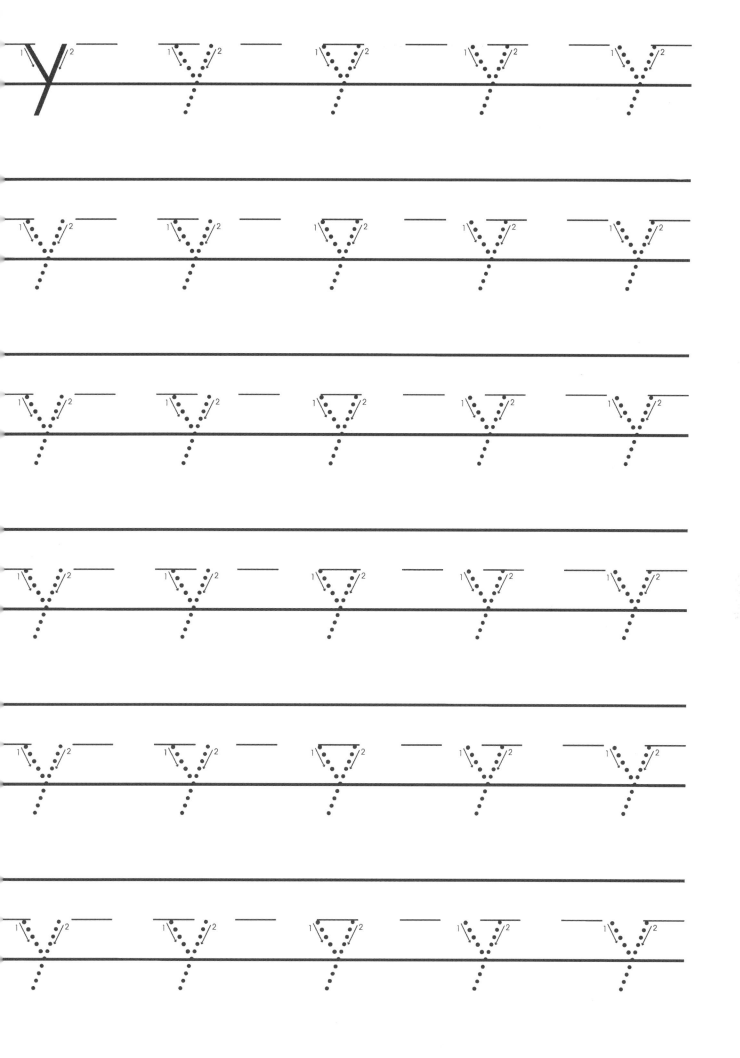

# The Latter Z

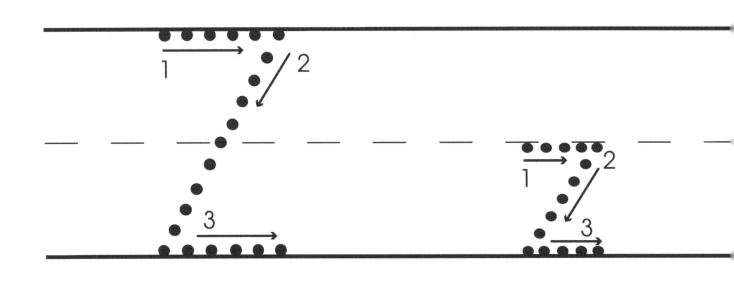

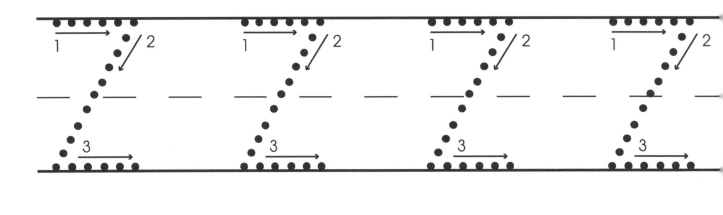

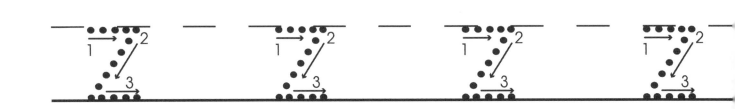

# Z is for

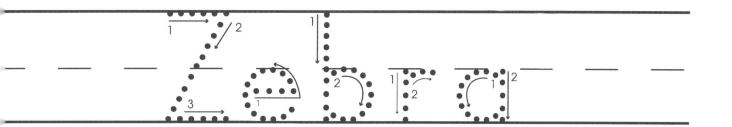

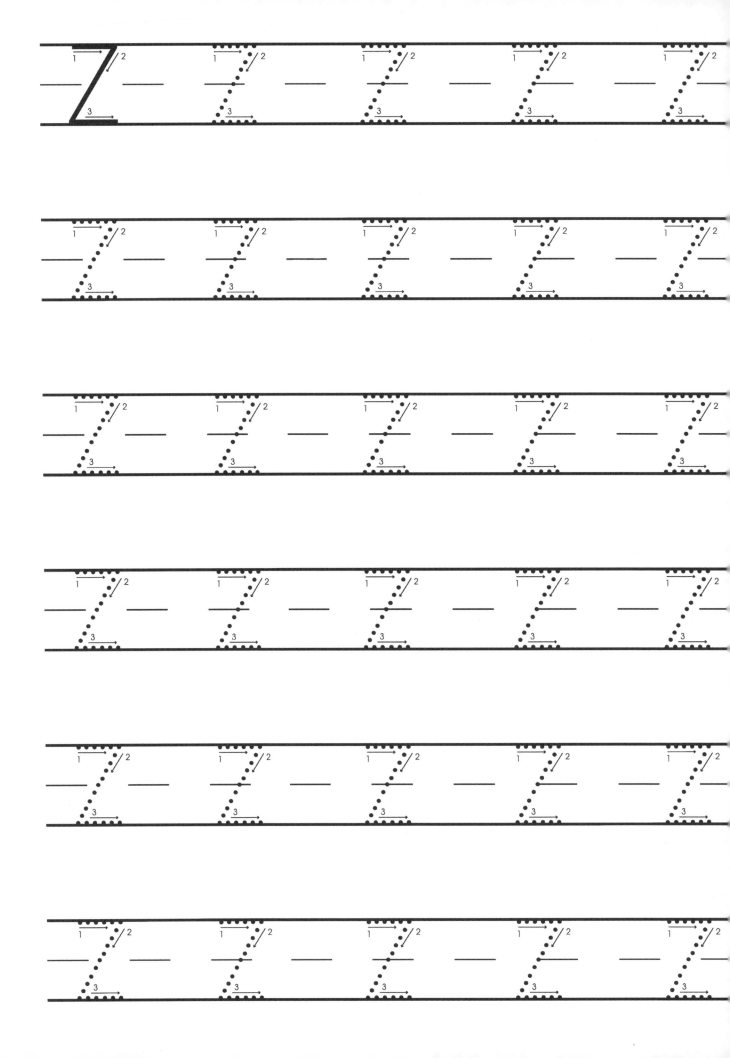

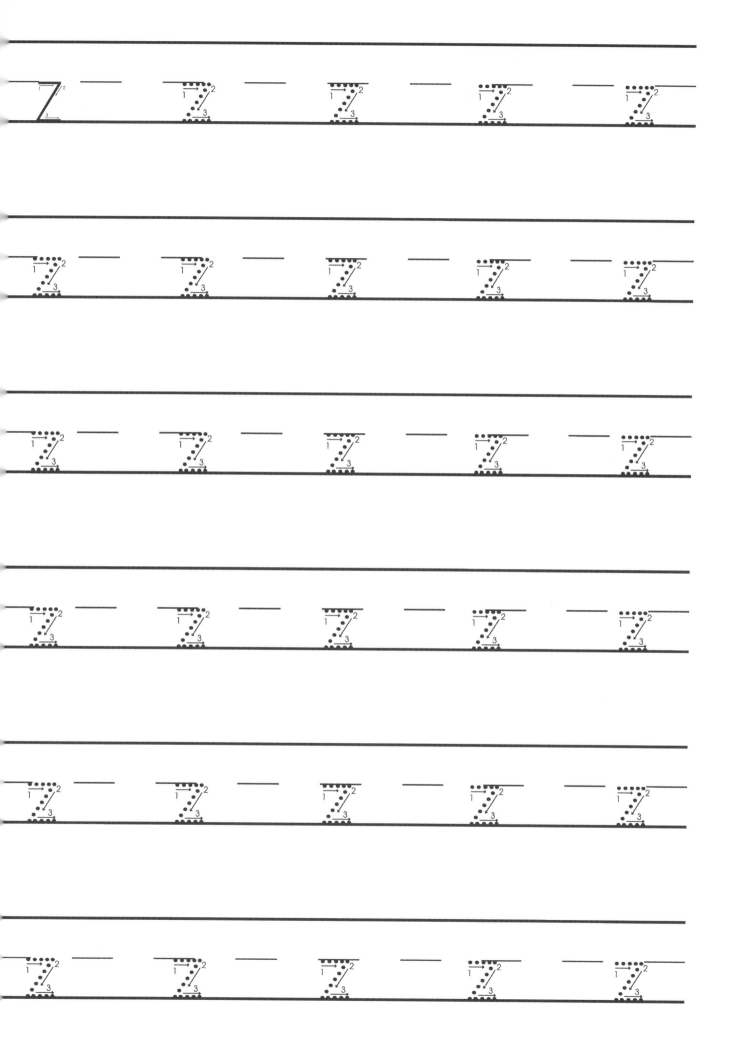

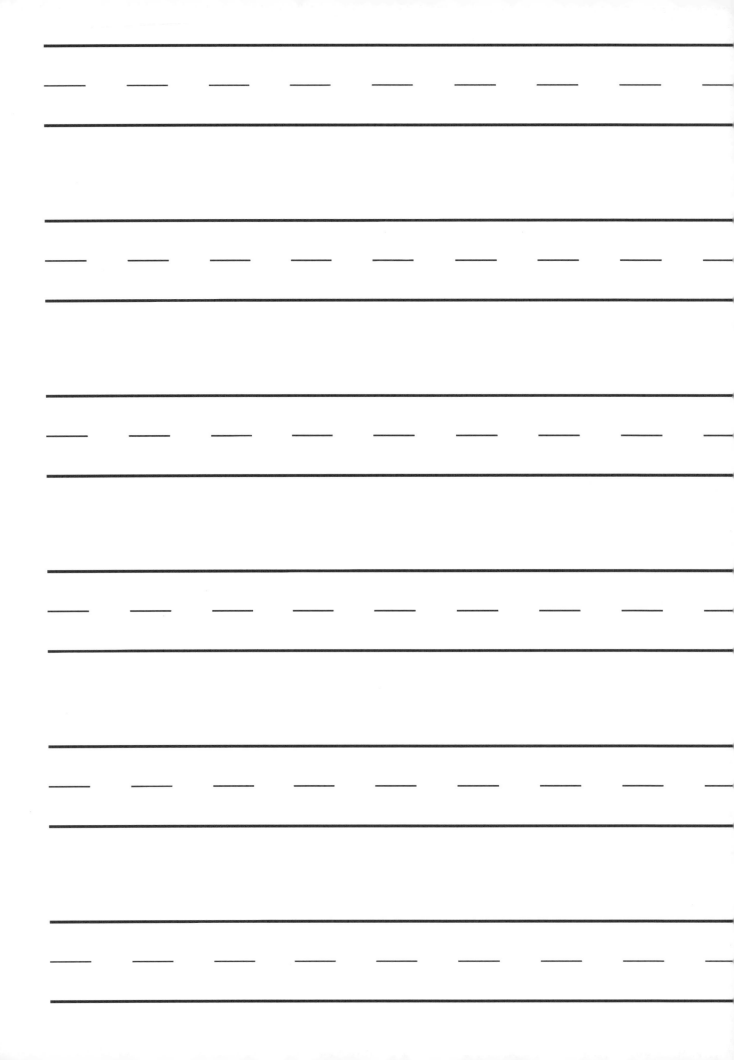

Made in the USA
Monee, IL
01 April 2020

24414165R00063